backdrop

the politics and personalities behind sexual orientation research

Gayle E. Pitman, Ph.D.

ACTIVE VOICE PRESS • SACRAMENTO, CA

www.activevoicepress.com

Cover art and book design by Amy Tackett

Libray of Congress Cataloging-in-Publication Data
Pitman, Gayle E.
        Backdrop: The politics and personalities behind sexual orientation research.

ISBN: 0615518125
ISBN-13: 9780615518121
LCCN: 2011913542

DEDICATION

To my students at Sacramento City College

CONTENTS

ACKNOWLEDGMENTS

When I decided that I was going to take the plunge and attempt to write a book, little did I know what a ride it would be. I took my sabbatical at Sacramento City College after my first year of being back to work full-time and juggling the demands of mothering my baby girl. I was feeling tired, stressed, and overwhelmed, and I thought that taking this sabbatical would kill two birds with one stone: it would buy me some time and flexibility with my schedule so I could get a better handle on the juggling act of life; and it would be the perfect opportunity to break ground on a writing project that I'd been thinking about for some time. I am extremely thankful to the Professional Standards Committee at Sacramento

City College for granting that sabbatical to me, and for having the trust and faith in me that I would produce a book that would have a positive impact on our students. I hope I have fulfilled that goal.

I really do think I'm blessed with the absolute best colleagues in the universe, and many of them deserve special thanks. Grace Austin, a colleague of mine in the psychology department, took my Psychology of Sexual Orientation class before I had even started considering writing a book, and she was instrumental in encouraging me to take the plunge into writing. Alan Keys provided very helpful feedback early in the writing process, primarily on the chapters focusing on the biological causes of sexual orientation. Angela Block and Norman Lorenz participated in an online consultation group when this book was in its formative stages, and they were instrumental in helping to shape the direction the book was going to go. Carl Sjovold provided some editorial advice during the end stages of this process, and he and I had numerous late-afternoon conversations that pushed me to think more deeply about some of the issues raised in this book. Sheley Little was extremely generous with her time in helping me deal with some very frustrating Microsoft Word formatting issues. I work in an environment that is so incredibly rich and fulfilling, and I am grateful to my colleagues for allowing me to tap into their expertise.

If it weren't for my students, this book would never have been written. My Psychology of Sexual Orientation students weren't the least bit shy about expressing their distaste for the text I was using in my class. Although listening to my students tell me "The textbook you chose for our class is really lousy!" isn't all that much fun, their feedback was coupled with the confidence that I could potentially take a better stab at the topic. A strong collective of students from that class gave me the encouragement that I needed to kick off this project: Kay Anderson, Thomas Costa, Kevin Erickson, Kelly Jordan, Tighearnan Lee, Mackenzie Lorenzato, Samantha Mello, Steven Nascimento, Irvis Orozco, Ash Pearsol, and Yumi Wilkerson. Later in this process, several students provided feedback and sparked my thinking through our numerous outside-of-class conversations: Keagan Andrews, Melissa Arvisais, Christine Brown-Kwaiser, Raechel Ibarra-Smith, Jessica Oler, and Adyn Wagoner. Special thanks to Adam Smith, who was extremely generous with his time in providing much-appreciated editorial feedback that helped give shape to the book.

Many, many other people provided encouragement, feedback, and fuel for the soul. Although she didn't know it at the time, an interview I had with Esther Rothblum changed the focus of this book dramatically, and her simple offhand comment ultimately made this a book that will probably be much more interesting to my students. Nanette Gartrell was very generous with her time early in the process, and although my interview with her didn't get included in the book, our conversation about her activist efforts to remove the homosexuality diagnosis from the DSM resulted in the inclusion of the chapter on Evelyn Hooker. Kim Renstrom, Jean Salfen, and Suzette Slusser all pitched in to give my eyes a vacation from the toils of proofreading, and each of them was vital in making this a clean, professional-looking publication. I am grateful to Julie Interrante for her friendship and for her level-headed, spiritually grounded guidance throughout this process. I am also indebted to Kira Stewart for supporting me throughout this creative journey, and for reminding me that Julia Cameron-style morning pages and artist dates really do lead to creative flow. I have found that to be absolutely true.

I want to give special thanks to a few people who are a part of the literary and self-publishing community in Sacramento. Many thanks to Christy Pinheiro, who was kind enough to send me a copy of two of her books, *The Step-By-Step Guide to Self-Publishing for Profit!* and *The Indie Book Reviewer Yellow Pages*. Being a newbie to the world of self-publishing, both of these books, as well as her personal advice, were incredibly helpful to me. Jeff Evans did an amazing job indexing this book, and I have a deep appreciation for the level of patience and attention to detail the indexing process must take. I am grateful to

Ken Hassman for gently and diplomatically discouraging me from trying to index the book myself. That simple piece of advice saved me a lot of unnecessary stress, and I could never have done the task justice.

My family is my lifeline, and one person in particular deserves special mention. Amy Tackett is my partner, soul mate, and resident graphic designer. Amy's invisible hand is behind every page of this book, and in many ways she is the Jill-of-all-trades. She created the cover art for my book that captured exactly the vision I had, and she did a beautiful job formatting the interior pages of the book. She willingly took up the slack at home and did the grunt work of household chores so my time would be freed up to work on the book. And she provided me with unwavering support throughout this entire process. I can't imagine any way of reciprocating what Amy has done for me, and the importance of her presence in my life.

Lastly, I want to thank all of the researchers who have the courage to devote their livelihood to the study of sexual orientation. It takes great courage and passion to focus on a topic that is so controversial, and the work that all of you do has changed the lives of many – myself included.

1

INTRODUCTION

I teach a class at Sacramento City College called "Psychology of Sexual Orientation." Only one other community college in California offers such a class, and only a handful of universities in California (and across the nation) include sexual orientation as a specific topic area in their psychology curriculum. Sexual orientation is known as a "specialty topic," a topic that is included as a course offering only if there is a resident expert on the faculty who specializes in that topic. Because it is such an idiosyncratic area, until recently there were no undergraduate-level textbooks focusing on lesbian, gay, bisexual, and transgender issues in psychology. So I limped along by cobbling together a "reader" comprised of articles – some academic, others more mainstream and accessible. I also assigned a non-academic book on LGBT issues for my students to read. And I fielded many, many complaints from students about these readings. *Boring. Dry. Too intellectual. Outdated.* These were the words I heard over and over again. And yet, our classroom discussions were quite the opposite. They were rich. They were lively. They were heated, emotional, challenging, upsetting, inspiring. They were real. "You should take what we talk about in class and write your own textbook," one of my students remarked one day, somewhat jokingly. I took her seriously.

Although I possess the qualifications to write a textbook on this topic, embarking on this process is not for the faint-hearted. A textbook is intended to be a comprehensive work, providing students with an overview of the theory and research focused on a particular subject area. It's a monumental task, to be sure, but I felt ready to take it on. In the fall of 2009, I took a sabbatical from my post as a full-time psychology professor, thinking that I could easily churn out a manuscript – particularly since I'd done so much of the legwork when I had put together the curriculum for the course. I'd also published several articles and book chapters on various topics involving sexual orientation, and I'd co-authored a textbook manuscript on the psychology of women. This sort of writing was not new to me. And yet, instead of churning out said manuscript, I sat staring at my computer screen for eight weeks straight. I couldn't figure out where to start. I had an outline that paralleled my class syllabus, and I was intimately familiar with the material I was planning to write about. So why couldn't I get it together and put pen to paper (or fingertips to computer keys)? I realized one day, when I was sitting yet again in front of a blank document on my computer screen, that it wasn't the sheer scope of the project that paralyzed me into inaction – it was that the idea of writing a textbook on such an inherently interesting topic bored the daylights out of me. Although I've learned some things from reading textbooks (and, in my student days, have stayed up quite late reading a textbook because of a test the next day), I've never stayed up until 3 o'clock in the morning because I just couldn't wait to finish reading a textbook. And I couldn't stomach the idea of requiring my students to pay $100 for a book that was boring – especially when the topic itself was so captivating.

On about the eighth week of this very frustrating bout of writer's block, I had a phone conversation about my book with Esther Rothblum, a psychologist and LGBT researcher at San Diego State University whose work I very much respect. As she was telling me about one of her early research studies, she said, in a somewhat offhand way, "There's a story behind every research study." When Esther said those words to me, it dawned on me that the book that needed to be written wasn't going to be a garden-variety textbook. Somehow, her comment shifted my perspective from that of an academic to that of a storyteller – and I realized that there was quite a story to be told. The path that LGBT research has taken, such as the work focusing on the biological basis of sexual orientation, has been like a series of slowly unfolding subplots, with lots of twists and developments. The people behind the research studies (both the scientists as well as the activists and reactionaries) bring humanity and character intrigue to the story. More often than not, the story ends not with a perky "happily ever after"-style ending, but instead with a series of unresolved questions. And all of the action takes place before the landscape of politics, religion, and moral values. I realized that I couldn't just dryly report the research findings – I wanted to tell the story behind research on sexual orientation.

So, given that insight, what do I hope to accomplish in this book? What I hope to argue in *Backdrop* is that, when it comes to sexual orientation research, we could potentially glean more powerful insights from the "backdrop" of politics and personalities behind the research than from the research itself. This viewpoint stands in stark contrast to the traditional stance of objectivity practiced in psychological science. Psychological research is, by definition, intended to be objective and unbiased. Researchers diligently follow the scientific method. They write up their research findings using the passive voice in order to achieve an objective tone. This objectivity is thought to be particularly important when it comes to highly controversial issues being studied. As a result, the people behind the research, as well as the baggage of values, feelings, experiences, and beliefs they carry, fade completely into the background, leaving the scientific findings to stand on their own. And yet, I really believe that there is a powerful wisdom that the human factor can reveal to us.

Here's an example of this. People who study sexual orientation are undoubtedly familiar with the work of Simon LeVay, Dean Hamer, J. Michael Bailey, Evelyn Hooker, and Gregory Herek, to name a few notable scientists in the field. Dean Hamer, for example, is known for his now-famous "gay gene" study, in which a portion of the X chromosome was linked to homosexuality in men. Evelyn Hooker is renowned for pioneering the notion that gay people are just as well-adjusted as heterosexuals. However, few people are aware of the details of these researchers' lives, the very personal factors that led them to study sexual orientation, and the impact their work has had on their lives. For example, if we examine how the scientific community and the public reacted to the work of three different researchers – Simon LeVay, J. Michael Bailey, and Dean Hamer – we can see that

being an out gay scientist, a heterosexual researcher, or a
scientist with an undisclosed sexual orientation provides
an important context for the work they did. While the
work of an openly gay scientist might be well-received by
the gay community, it might be viewed with suspicion by
religious organizations and anti-gay activists. In contrast,
the findings of a heterosexual researcher might be seen as
suspect by the gay community, because of the researcher's
out-group status. And a researcher with an undisclosed
orientation? While avoiding disclosure of one's personal
status might provide a shield from personal attacks, the
veil of objectivity comes at a cost. Knowing something
about the people behind the research can provide us with a
more nuanced understanding of sexual orientation issues.

Three different stories are addressed in this book.
The first three chapters of "The Biology Story" chronicle
three major studies supporting a biological basis for
homosexuality: Simon LeVay's brain structure research,
J. Michael Bailey's heritability studies, and Dean Hamer's
famous "gay gene" study. A fourth study, conducted by
Lisa Diamond, offers a counter-narrative to the typical
coming-out story by investigating the "outlier" experiences
of women and bisexuals – experiences that don't fall
predictably along the bell curve and that challenge the
"born that way" theory of homosexuality.

"The Gender Story," the second major storyline
in the book, uses research on intersex and transgender

identities to address the question of whether gender identity is biologically hard-wired or socially constructed and imprinted. Several researchers – John Money, Milton Diamond, J. Michael Bailey, and Alice Dreger – are profiled in this section, all of whom endured significant personal and professional consequences for "going off-message" – that is, for developing or endorsing theories that were unpopular or that contradicted the official party line.

Lastly, "The Activism Story," a three-chapter sequence, profiles the lives, personalities, and work of Evelyn Hooker and Gregory Herek, both of whom have worked tirelessly to advocate for LGBT rights – and both have been accused of being "activist researchers" by members of anti-gay organizations. This story culminates with a discussion of the major historical and current LGBT public policy issues, such as the "don't ask, don't tell" military policy, employment rights for public schoolteachers, sodomy laws, and marriage equality rights. The final chapter of this story also gives voice to three major groups involved in these issues: the pro-gay researchers who have advocated for these rights; the anti-gay religious groups who claim to adhere to a God-dictated moral code; and the "shadow characters" who exist on the fringes of the LGBT community, and who aren't necessarily on board with the mainstream gay activist agenda.

So the story begins. Once upon a time . . . .

PART I

THE BIOLOGY STORY

2

THE OUT GAY SCIENTIST

What makes people gay? This is probably one of the most frequently-asked – and most controversial – questions regarding sexual orientation. Although homosexual behavior in men and women took place even in ancient cultures, the idea of a homosexual or heterosexual orientation wasn't introduced until the 19th century. From that point forward, two major views of homosexuality prevailed until the end of the 20th century – the religious view and the Freudian/psychodynamic view.

According to the religious view, homosexuality is a sin – a chosen lifestyle propelled by the devil. While some religions, such as Islam, view homosexuality as punishable by death, others adopt the view of "hate the sin, not the sinner" – while homosexuality is a sinful behavior, people who engage in homosexual acts are still loved by God. In either case, people choose to engage in homosexual behaviors, according to this view. In religions that utilize the Old Testament, numerous biblical passages are often quoted to support this view. Not surprisingly, most LGBT activists believe that the religious view is homophobic and ignorant, and that it dangerously reinforces the idea that homosexuality is a choice.

The second view, popularized by contemporaries of Freud, suggests that homosexuality is not necessarily a choice, but rather the result of a disruption in the child's developmental path. Interestingly, Freud himself had a mixture of views regarding homosexuality. For one thing, he believed that all humans begin life with a bisexual disposition, and that a heterosexual orientation results from the appropriate resolution of the phallic and genital stages of psychosexual development. Freud viewed homosexuality as a deviation from this developmental path, although he vacillated throughout his career about whether homosexuality represented a normal or pathological sexual variation. However, his general feeling was that homosexuality, while an atypical developmental path, is *not* a form of pathology, nor should (or can) it be corrected through conversion therapy. In his now-famous "Letter to an American Mother," a response to a woman whose son was gay, Freud stated the following:

Homosexuality is assuredly no advantage, but it is nothing to be ashamed of, no vice, no degradation; it cannot be classified as an illness; we consider it to be a variation of the sexual function, produced by a certain arrest of sexual development. Many highly respectable individuals of ancient and modern times have been homosexuals, several of the greatest men among them. (Plato, Michelangelo, Leonardo da Vinci, etc.). It is a great injustice to persecute homosexuality as a crime —and a cruelty, too. If you do not believe me, read the books of Havelock Ellis. By asking me if I can help [your son], you mean, I suppose, if I can abolish homosexuality and make normal heterosexuality take its place. The answer is, in a general way we cannot promise to achieve it. In a certain number of cases we succeed in developing the blighted germs of heterosexual tendencies, which are present in every homosexual; in the majority of cases it is no more possible. It is a question of the quality and the age of the individual. The result of treatment cannot be predicted. What analysis can do for your son runs in a different line. If he is unhappy, neurotic, torn by conflicts, inhibited in his social life, analysis may bring him harmony, peace of mind, full efficiency, *whether he remains homosexual or gets changed* (emphasis added).[1]

Not only did Freud view homosexuality as a "variation of the sexual function," he also believed that conversion therapy was generally useless. In fact, at one point in his career Freud noted that the majority of homosexuals wanted to change their sexual orientation not because they truly wanted to be heterosexual, but because they feared social disapproval – a weak justification, in Freud's mind.

Oddly enough, later psychoanalysts, deftly cherry-picking from Freud's work, have argued that homosexuality is unnatural and pathological, and that it can and should be changed. In the 1960s, two psychoanalysts emerged to promote the homosexuality-as-pathology theory – the first being Irving Bieber, the second being Charles Socarides. Bieber is probably best-known for his nine-year study of 106 gay men titled *Homosexuality: A Psychoanalytic Study of Male Homosexuals,*[2] which utilized Freud's psychosexual theory to support the idea of homosexuality as an abnormality. Both Bieber and Socarides were heavily involved in attempts to preserve homosexuality as a psychiatric disorder in the *Diagnostic and Statistical Manual of Mental Disorders* (DSM), the diagnostic authority commonly used by mental health practitioners. More notably, they were the premier advocates of the use of reparative therapy to "cure" homosexuality, which, in the pre-Stonewall 1960s, was likely seen as a ray of hope to many homosexuals.

The argument essentially goes as follows: According to Bieber and Socarides, healthy male development involves moving away from mother and identifying with father. A young boy's sense of masculinity is very weak and fragile, and father must shore up his son's fragile masculine identity by introducing him to the realities of the outside world (as my students would say, fathers need to teach their sons to "man-up"). More importantly, the father must prevent the mother from emotionally asphyxiating the child (in Freudian terms, this is referred to as "mother-infant symbiosis"). Again, as my students would say, "being a mama's boy will make him go soft." In fact, in order to become a man, a boy needs to separate from his mother and reject femininity. In this view, homosexuality and masculinity are completely mutually exclusive, and gay men are essentially "gender inverts." Heterosexuality is the ultimate sign that a man has developed a healthy sense of masculinity; in yin-yang form, masculinity and femininity complement one another without a boy's masculinity being overtaken by the feminine.

The idea that boys need to absorb male energy in order to become masculine isn't necessarily a new or novel concept. Interestingly, a number of ancient and contemporary cultures do in fact have "manning-up" rituals – although ironically, these rituals almost always involve some form of male homosexual activity. While neo-Freudians view homosexuality as a sign of masculine development gone awry, other cultures see homosexuality as a means to a masculine end. In ancient Greece, for example, sexual relations between boys and men (known as "pederasty") were relatively common. Some scholars have considered this homosexual activity to be a masculine rite of passage. Others have characterized male homosexual behavior as a path towards enlightenment; in order to gain enlightenment in the Greek masculine aristocracy, one must seek another male, as females were not considered to be members of the "enlightened" race. A more contemporary example is seen in the Etoro of New Guinea, where men are considered to become virile by receiving sperm, filled with life-force, of other members. Boys spend their teen and young adult years engaging in homosexual activities with older men before marrying. Here in the United States, these activities would clearly be characterized as pedophilia, which is culturally taboo as well as punishable by law.

Going back to homosexuality-as-pathology: The American Psychiatric Association introduced the diagnosis of "homosexuality" in the DSM in 1952, and for the next several decades, reparative therapy was *the* approach to dealing with homosexuality. During the same general time period, in 1957, Evelyn Hooker had published her now-famous study "The Adjustment of the Male Overt Homosexual," which presented a completely different viewpoint that "homosexuals were not inherently abnormal and that there was no difference between homosexual and heterosexual men in terms of pathology."[3] Although Hooker's research eventually served as the basis for removing the diagnosis of homosexuality from the DSM in 1973, the scientific community was slow to warm up to her work. In the meantime, homosexual patients were subjected to all sorts of "therapeutic" techniques, including Freudian-style psychoanalysis, involving endless hours of ramblings involving the patient's mother; Pavlovian-inspired aversive conditioning, including shock therapy and nausea-inducing drugs; and the sex therapies of Masters and Johnson, the famed husband-and-wife research team. Hormone injections, testicular transplants, and chemical castration rounded out the more barbaric treatments used.

These theories and techniques were widely accepted and used until the 1970s, on the heels of the Stonewall riots and the birth of the gay and lesbian liberation movement. Gay activist groups, following in the footsteps of civil rights activists, began utilizing more radical, in-your-face strategies such as marches, rioting, and demonstrations – and the American Psychiatric

Association became a target of the movement. Activists began protesting lectures by psychiatrists and other professionals who espoused the homosexuality-as-pathology viewpoint. These efforts included picketing the 1968 American Medical Association (AMA) meeting in San Francisco, where Charles Socarides was speaking. Later, in 1970, activists disrupted Irving Bieber's talk at the American Psychiatric Association meeting in San Francisco by using guerilla theater techniques. In 1973, the APA Committee on Nomenclature, chaired by Robert Spitzer, voted to remove homosexuality from the DSM. However, the committee, along with many other psychiatrists and mental health professionals, still had difficulty supporting the idea that all homosexuality is a normal sexual variation, and in 1980 the diagnosis of "ego-dystonic homosexuality"– homosexuality that is unwanted and distressing – was included in the DSM. It wasn't until 1986 that all forms of homosexuality were removed from the DSM. Ego-dystonic homosexuality, however, remains a diagnostic category in the World Health Organization's International Classification of Diseases (ICD-10).

The APA's shift from "homosexuality-as-pathology" to "homosexuality as normal sexual variation" caused reverberations throughout the scientific community, and it marked a shift in the type of research that was being conducted on homosexuality. Most of these efforts focused on the causes of homosexuality; if homosexuality is a normal variation of human sexuality, then perhaps there is a biological basis to it. A multitude of research efforts began to fan out in several different directions. One of those directions involved chronicling homosexuality (or non-heterosexuality) in the animal kingdom. Amazon River dolphins, bonobos, African and Asian male elephants, fruit flies, snow monkeys, lions, and sheep, among others, were offered up as examples of species who engage in normal variations of sexual behavior. Another research direction involved the "androgen theory" of homosexuality – the idea that a particular family of sex hormones that contributes to the development of male sexual characteristics may influence sexual orientation. For example, male rats will exhibit lordosis (receptive sexual behavior typical of females) if castrated and administered female sex hormones, and females will exhibit mounting through similar manipulation of sex hormones.[4] Still another research direction involved identifying the "gay brain structure" – areas in the brain which differ between homosexuals and heterosexuals.

Enter Simon LeVay. LeVay, who is himself gay, originally began his career as a vision researcher. He joined the famed research team of David Hubel and Torsten Wiesel at Harvard University in 1971, and in 1984 he went to the Salk Institute to head up his own vision laboratory. However, his research took a significant detour in 1990, when his partner Richard died after a four-year struggle with AIDS. LeVay offered the following quote in an interview in *Discover* magazine: "Richard and I had spent 21 years together. It was while looking after him that I decided I wanted to do something different with my life. You realize life is short, and you have to think about what is important to you and what isn't. I had an emotional need to do something more personal, something connected with my gay identity."[5]

In 1991, shortly after his partner's death, LeVay set out to test the "gay brain structure" theory. For more than a century, theories have abounded regarding brain differences between males and females. Since the 1980s, researchers had documented several areas of sexual dimorphism – physical differences between males and females. Many examples of sexual dimorphism are obvious – for example, males tend to be taller than females; males tend to have more facial hair than females; females tend to have a higher body fat ratio than males; and so on. Some of this research goes beyond the obviously visible differences and chronicles differences in male and female brains. The sexual dimorphism of the brain is what LeVay was interested in. What LeVay found to be most compelling was the work of Laura Allen and Roger Gorski, which indicated that a sex difference existed in the size of three areas of the brain – the anterior commissure, the corpus callosum, and an area they called INAH-3 – the interstitial nucleus of the anterior hypothalamus. It was this third area – the INAH-3 – that LeVay took an interest in. Allen and Gorski found that INAH-3 was more than twice as large in men as in women.[6] LeVay took Allen and Gorski's research a step further and hypothesized that the size of brain structures might vary with sexual orientation as well as sex. Operating on the assumption that gay men might, biologically speaking, be more like heterosexual women than heterosexual men (a concept sometimes referred to as the "gender inversion" theory of homosexuality), LeVay asked himself whether differences that show up between men and women would also show up between straight and gay men. More specifically, LeVay postulated that the size of INAH-3 would be correlated with sexual orientation – larger in heterosexual men and lesbian women, and smaller in heterosexual women and gay men.

The INAH-3 is a tiny area of the hypothalamus, too small to be observed through MRI or other imaging technology. In order to conduct this research, LeVay autopsied the brains of 41 people – 19 homosexual men, 16 heterosexual men, and 6 women. To reduce bias, each brain sample was numerically coded to conceal whether its donor was straight or gay. When LeVay analyzed the results, he saw a robust difference: straight men had

INAH-3s twice the size of gay men's. In an interview in *Discover* magazine, LeVay shared his reactions to his findings: "I was almost in a state of shock. I took a walk by myself on the cliffs over the ocean. I sat for half an hour just thinking what this might mean."[7]

While LeVay was conducting his study, a number of other research efforts documenting a possible biological basis to homosexuality were quietly taking place. All of this research was published in the early 1990s – ironically, at the height of the "don't ask, don't tell" controversy. Shortly after LeVay published his findings, another highly-publicized study, this one conducted by Michael Bailey and Richard Pillard, hit the research scene. In this study, Bailey (discussed later in this volume) and Pillard looked at the concordance rates of homosexuality between male identical twins, fraternal twins, and adoptive (genetically unrelated) brothers (meaning, if one identical twin is gay, the likelihood that the other identical twin is gay as well). Since identical twins share identical genetic information, this is a useful way to study the heritability of a trait. In this study, 52% of identical twin brothers were gay, compared to 22% of nonidentical twins and 11% of adoptive genetically unrelated brothers, suggesting at least a moderate biological basis to homosexuality.[8] Later, in 1996, Ray Blanchard proposed what is called the "fraternal birth order effect," or "older brother effect." According to this theory, the more older brothers a man has, the greater likelihood that he will be gay.[9] And in 1993, Dean Hamer's "gay gene" study – the one to hit the media in a firestorm – identified the Xq28 area on the X chromosome as a possible marker for homosexuality in men (to be discussed in more detail in this volume).[10] Clearly, this groundswell of research was forcing the "homosexuality-as-pathology" perspective to fade into the background.

LeVay's findings were published in 1991 in *Science*, which is one of the most prestigious (and widely read) journals in the scientific community. Immediately LeVay found himself at the epicenter of controversy. Within a week after publication, LeVay was thrust into the media spotlight, appearing on *Donahue*, the *Oprah Winfrey Show*, the *MacNeill/Lehrer Report*, and *Nightline*. He gave numerous interviews for newspapers and popular magazines. And LeVay got it from all directions – starting with the scientific community. LeVay was criticized by numerous scientists for using a small sample size, for adopting a binary view of homosexuality and not acknowledging bisexuality as a valid orientation, and for excluding female homosexuality. Two other criticisms are of note. As Charles Socarides was quick to point out, all of the male homosexuals who were studied had died of AIDS. Because of this confound, it is impossible to distinguish whether the size of INAH-3 differed because of sexual orientation, or because of

HIV infection. For example, men with AIDS can have decreased testosterone levels as a side effect of treatment or as a result of opportunistic infections, and decreased testosterone levels might be associated with (or influence) the size of brain regions.[11] (In LeVay's defense, most of the straight men had died of AIDS as well, which would have eliminated the HIV confound.) Second, how subjects were identified as gay or heterosexual is questionable. Since the participants were deceased, they couldn't self-identify as gay, bisexual, heterosexual, or otherwise, so alternative corroboration needed to be used. All of the men classified as homosexual were identified through hospital records that indicated whether they had engaged in sexual activity with another man. Since all of these subjects had AIDS, hospitals would have gathered this information in order to better understand whether sexual activity was the route of HIV transmission. Some individuals who were gay might have been classified as heterosexual, and heterosexual men who had some form of sexual activity with another man would have been counted as gay.

Scientific scrutiny is part of the game, and while LeVay was prepared for a certain degree of scientific criticism, being pummeled with questions probably caught him off-guard. He was also likely caught off-guard by the fact that emotionally charged responses to his work were coming from both anti-gay activists *and* the gay community. The anti-gay activists probably didn't surprise him – it's to be expected that they would argue that homosexuality is a sin and a choice, and that no matter what the research reveals, the Bible trumps science. The response from the gay community, however, was much more equivocal. Many, many people wrote to LeVay thanking him for his work. "Many gay men sent my study to their parents, particularly if they were somewhat estranged from them," says LeVay. "And parents, in turn, wrote to say the study helped them understand their kids."[12] However, other responses from the gay community were not so positive. For one thing, because LeVay classified his participants as either homosexual or heterosexual, bisexuality as a distinct identity essentially fell through the cracks. In fact, for the record, LeVay reinforced the "one-drop rule" by including a bisexual-identified man in the homosexual group. Second, reminiscent of the controversy surrounding research on sex differences in the brain, LeVay was accused of pathologizing gay men – that their INAH-3s are "less than" those of heterosexual men because they are comparatively smaller and similar to those of females. Taking this critique of the gender inversion theory a step further, LeVay was accused of providing the neo-Freudians with biological ammunition by "painting gay men as women in disguise."[12]And, in an even more damning accusation, critics insinuated that LeVay was part of a larger group of eugenics researchers

– people who were invested in weeding sexual minorities out of the gene pool.[13]

One of the most valid criticisms that persisted for years was that LeVay was the only researcher to connect INAH-3 with homosexuality in males. In order for a scientific finding to gain credibility, it needs to be replicated – to be repeated by a different researcher with a different subject pool. Throughout the 1990s, when research on the biological basis was exploding, nothing emerged that replicated LeVay's INAH-3 finding. William Byne, a researcher at Mount Sinai School of Medicine, was originally one of the skeptics. His biggest concern was that AIDS caused by homosexual behavior might have different effects on the brain than AIDS caused by IV drug use. However, in a series of studies he conducted, he amassed powerful evidence in support of LeVay's work. For one thing, he repeated Allen and Gorski's finding that INAH-3 is larger in heterosexual men than in heterosexual women. He demonstrated that, in rats, the chemical composition of INAH-3 is similar to that of the sexually dimorphic nucleus, an area associated with sexuality and that is twice as large in males as in females. He administered male sex hormones to female rhesus monkeys and found that INAH-3 in these monkeys was larger than that in a control group of monkeys who weren't given the hormones. And – probably his most important finding – he studied the brains of heterosexual men, heterosexual women, and gay men, and repeated LeVay's finding.[14] Replication is the gold standard of scientific research, and LeVay's work has met that standard.

Why is this biologically-based line of inquiry so powerfully controversial? Those who are more accepting of gay and lesbian individuals tend to adopt a biologically-based view of homosexuality, whereas those who are less tolerant or believe homosexuality is wrong tend to adopt a religious, choice-based, or damaged-childhood perspective. As a result, LeVay's research has found its way to the front of the battle lines. His research, along with the work of Michael Bailey and Dean Hamer, has been cited in numerous court cases involving same-sex marriage and other forms of protection against discrimination. In 1994, LeVay testified on behalf of the plaintiff in *Merino v. Boy Scouts* regarding their policies regarding homosexuality.[15] His work continues to be cited by researchers and by gay and lesbian activists. Yet his work has probably had the most significant impact at the ground level. A 1994 *Advocate* survey found that 90% of gay men surveyed said they had been born that way, and 4% said choice was involved; of lesbians, almost half said they were born gay, 28% thought that environment (particularly childhood) played a role, and 15% said choice was involved.[16] Quite a difference from the days of Irving Bieber, Charles Socarides, and the homosexuality diagnosis.

And yet, LeVay decided to move on. Shortly after the publication of his study, LeVay left his post at the Salk Institute and hasn't conducted research on homosexuality since then. In 1993 he co-founded the West Hollywood Institute of Gay and Lesbian Education, which offers courses on a range of topics related to sexual orientation. He continued to author books, popular articles, and opinion pieces, many of which focus on the biological basis of homosexuality, but which also detour to the unlikely topics of Parkinson's disease, extraterrestrial life, science fiction, and earthquakes and volcanoes. In defense of his decision to abandon sexual orientation research, LeVay commented,

> Science alone can only go so far in rolling back prejudice, because prejudice is based in irrationality and can't always be approached with rational arguments. There's a human dimension to it that also needs to be addressed. Besides, on a purely moral level, there's no justification for discrimination against homosexuality, regardless of its causation. Even if homosexuality were not biological even if it were a conscious choice there would still be grounds to respect gay people, because of our beliefs about people's right to privacy and freedom of action and because of the contributions gays and lesbians make to society.[17]

LeVay went on to say, "I realized, when I'd come to the end of my life, I wanted to feel I'd done something to give me personal satisfaction. It's not entirely rational, but a lot of gay men are propelled into activism as a result of their experiences with AIDS. Richard and I were a couple, a hardworking doctor and a scientist, but not really involved in the gay community. His illness changed that."[18] The loss of his partner propelled him into his INAH-3 research, and the INAH-3 research allowed him to rise to a different level of activism.

————————

So LeVay has moved on, but what of the "homosexuality-as-pathology" theorists? Irving Bieber died in 1991 – the same year LeVay's study was published in *Science*. Charles Socarides, on the other hand, was a vocal critic of LeVay's research, dismantling his findings in his book *Homosexuality: A Freedom Too Far* (1995), among other places. Interestingly, Socarides' son Richard is openly gay, having served on the White House Task Force for Lesbian and Gay Issues during the Clinton administration. In an interview between LeVay and Socarides for the British documentary *Born That Way?*, Socarides became enraged when asked what had caused his son to become homosexual. His response: "How would you like it if I asked you about your HIV status?"[19]

Later, toeing the homosexuality-as-pathology party line, Socarides conceded that his divorce from his second wife likely rendered him physically and emotionally unavailable to his son, depriving his son of the opportunity to absorb male energy and resulting in Richard's homosexuality. Socarides held strongly to this view and continued to advocate for the merits of reparative therapy until his death in 2005.

Yet the reparative-therapy movement persists, and in fact has undergone a bit of a renaissance. In 1992, Socarides and Bieber co-founded the National Association of Research and Therapy of Homosexuality (NARTH), an organization that advocates the use of reparative therapy to "cure" the unnatural state of homosexuality. One of their co-founders was a relative newcomer on the scene named Joseph Nicolosi, who could be characterized as "the new Socarides." Nicolosi is the author of *Reparative Therapy of Male Homosexuality*,[20] which is the seminal textbook used by therapists who treat homosexuality. Staying true to his neo-Freudian forefathers, Nicolosi offers the following contemporary "manning-up" (and totally stereotypical) suggestions for helping men overcome their unwanted homosexuality:

1. participate in sports activities;

2. (avoid activities considered of interest to

homosexuals; such [as] art museums, opera, symphonies;

3. avoid women unless it is for romantic contact;

4. increase time spent with heterosexual men in order to learn to mimic heterosexual male ways of walking, talking, and interacting with other heterosexual men;

5. attend church and join a men's church group;

6. attend a reparative therapy group to discuss progress, or slips back into homosexuality;

7. become more assertive with women through flirting and dating;

8. begin heterosexual dating;

9. engage in heterosexual intercourse;

10. enter into heterosexual marriage; and

11. father children.[21]

LeVay's research marked the beginning of a new focus on the biological basis of sexual orientation. Simultaneously, the establishment of NARTH and the subsequent publication of Nicolosi's book marked the beginning (or resurgence) of a coexisting pathological view of homosexuality. Both movements have gained significant momentum over the last two decades, creating the perfect storm of political controversy. Although NARTH was in its infancy in 1992, it has proven to be a formidable rival in the eyes of the gay and lesbian community. And while LeVay may have been the first LGBT researcher in recent years to weather the storm of scientific and public scrutiny, his experience foreshadowed what was yet to come.

3

THE VEIL OF OBJECTIVITY

It is hard to do sex research. It's even more difficult if the topic has anything to do with sexual orientation. It is the stuff of social movements, anarchy, and revolt. Funding for sex research, particularly when the focus is on LGBT issues, is sparse; unless the topic is HIV/AIDS, most research on LGBT issues is funded through small grants, or not funded at all. If the research is at all politically and socially controversial – and sex certainly falls under that category – funding agencies are unlikely to award money for the work.

Alfred Kinsey, the famed sex researcher of the 1940s, broke the mold by securing funding through the renowned Rockefeller Foundation to conduct large-

scale surveys on male and female sexual behavior. In his
empirical work and in his personal life, he challenged
conventional values about sexuality. His work heralded
the possibility of establishing sexology as an empirical
science, in contrast to the psychoanalytic tradition of the
time. His work instantly became the focus of massive
media coverage, and his books hit the bestseller lists.
And yet, despite the popularity of his work, Kinsey
became the focus of unrelenting attacks from religious
leaders, other scientists, and politicians. In 1954, after a
congressional investigation regarding their support of
Kinsey's work, the Rockefeller Foundation terminated
their funding commitment.[22]

Fifty years later, sex researchers still have
difficulty securing large-scale funding, particularly
from government agencies. Even William Masters and
Virginia Johnson, the famed husband-and-wife research
team, never received any funding for their work from
government agencies – their work was deemed too
controversial. In fact, their early work – which is now
so widely taught in human sexuality courses – was
rejected by scientific journals for being "pornographic."
Like Kinsey, Masters and Johnson were revered by the
public and reviled by the scientific community, religious
leaders, and medical professionals. Masters and Johnson
even went so far as to send their children to boarding
school so they would be protected from harassment.[23]

Throughout their careers, their work and their personal lives were under constant scrutiny.

So how on earth did funding and institutional support get secured from the National Institutes of Health, the world's largest biomedical research facility, for a study investigating the presence of a "gay gene"? The idea that sexual orientation is biologically based is quite controversial, and given the history of sex research funding, you'd think that a government agency as large as the NIH wouldn't want to touch it with a ten-foot pole. Moreover, the competition for NIH funding is fierce – for a tenure-track academic establishing a research program, an NIH grant pretty much guarantees tenure. To secure a large-scale grant for a "gay gene" study, you'd have to have an ironclad scientific pedigree and extremely savvy grant-writing skills. Given the scrutiny Kinsey's and Masters and Johnson's personal lives underwent, a squeaky-clean personal history probably wouldn't hurt. And, given that 10% of NIH funds support projects conducted by NIH researchers, insider status probably wouldn't hurt either.

Dean Hamer was that insider. Touting that ironclad scientific pedigree, Hamer received a bachelor's degree from Trinity College and his Ph.D. from Harvard University. Shortly after receiving his doctoral degree, he secured a post at the NIH and eventually became the Chief of the Section on Gene Structure and Regulation in the Laboratory of Biochemistry of the National Cancer Institute, where his research was anything but LGBT-related. In fact, his path was strikingly similar to that of Simon LeVay. Like LeVay, Hamer spent a large part of his career researching an obscure topic – in his case, that topic was "the regulation of metallothionein (MT) gene transcription by heavy metal ions."[24] While this might have been a topic of interest to other researchers, it would never make the cover of *Time* magazine. After 20 years of being a scientist and 10 years of studying MT gene transcription, Hamer was no longer inspired by his research, and he experienced an internal struggle regarding the meaning of his work. As he quotes in his book, *The Science of Desire*, "I had learned quite a bit about how genes work in individual cells, but I knew little about what makes people tick."[25]

Of course, this wasn't just an intellectual shift – Hamer's shift had a personal component to it. As he stated in a 1997 interview with *Discover* magazine, "I had a lot of friends with AIDS. One died within a year, others stayed healthy. It seemed random."[26] Wanting to find meaning in these experiences, Hamer began the transition from metallothionein to sexual orientation. So, by day, Hamer was dutifully conducting his abstruse NIH work, but by night, he was reading Darwin's *Descent of Man, and Selection in Relation to Sex* – and realizing that (1) sexuality likely has a significant genetic component, and (2) that he would never, ever be bored with the emotionally and politically charged topics of genetics and sexuality. This, as Hamer would later come to realize, was probably the understatement of the century.

While continuing his work at the NIH, Hamer underwent a six-month crash course in sexuality and behavioral genetics. At the time, there wasn't a large body of literature to master. In 1991, the year Simon LeVay published his INAH-3 findings, a Medline search Hamer conducted yielded only 14 articles. Fewer than half were actual research articles based on experiments – the rest were reviews, speculation, and "polemics." Most of the empirical work at that time had been conducted by two researchers, Richard Pillard and Michael Bailey. Their most groundbreaking work, as described earlier, was on the heritability of sexual orientation, and Hamer was very impressed with their twin studies. Pillard was no longer doing research, but Bailey was, and he agreed to meet with Hamer while in town for the APA convention. This encounter likely marked Hamer's induction into the LGBT research clique.

How does a man who works at the National Cancer Institute conduct "gay gene" research – especially if his 10-year track record involved studying metallothionein? For that matter, how does *anybody* get funded by a major government institution to do "gay gene" research? In his book, *The Science of Desire*, Hamer diplomatically described the grant approval process. Because studying the genetics of homosexuality would require the collection of a large data set, Hamer reasoned, it would make sense to get as much out of the data as he could. Ultimately, Hamer decided to focus on genetic variation in the progression of the HIV virus, using Kaposi's sarcoma in particular as a benchmark. The focus on Kaposi's sarcoma, a form of cancer, provided the tie-in to Hamer's post at the National Cancer Institute. Hamer also wanted to look at the genetics of alcoholism and other mental health issues in association with sexual orientation. Looking at the title of Hamer's proposal, one would never guess that a genetic marker for sexual orientation was being studied: "Genetic Factors and Interrelationships for Sexual Orientation, HIV Progression, and Kaposi's Sarcoma, Alcoholism and Related Psychopathology, and Histocompatibility Antigens."[27] Angela Pattatucci, one of Hamer's research colleagues, put it more bluntly: "We quietly convinced the federal government to approve funding support for this study."[28] Essentially, the research team wrapped the "gay gene" component of the study up in a blanket of legitimacy and smuggled it through.

To investigate the genetics of sexual orientation, Hamer and his colleagues conducted what is referred to as a linkage study, which investigates parts of chromosomes (called loci) that are inherited jointly.

Hamer and his colleagues began by tracing the lineages of gay men. In his sample of 76 gay brothers and their families, gay men had more gay male uncles and cousins on the mother's side of the family than on the father's, a phenomenon referred to as sex linkage. This prompted Hamer to look more closely at the sex chromosomes – the X and Y chromosomes that determine gender – as a possible contributor to sexual orientation. Since this study suggested that male homosexuality might be inherited from mothers, the researchers zeroed in on the X chromosome. Gay brothers who showed this maternal pedigree were then tested for X chromosome linkage – in other words, whether a marker that is linked to the X chromosome was common to these gay brothers. Thirty-three of the forty sibling pairs tested (82.5%) shared a marker on the X chromosome in an area called Xq28. No other region on the X chromosome showed a strong linkage. According to Hamer, "This is by far the strongest evidence to date that there is a genetic component to sexual orientation. We've identified a portion of the genome associated with it."[29]

When it came to publication, Hamer reached for the stars. *Science* is one of the world's most prestigious journals, covering a wide range of scientific disciplines and enjoying a readership of about one million people. Not only was the article accepted for publication, but the editors put it on what is referred to as "fast-track" for publication. Usually, once an article is accepted for publication, it takes many, many months before it is actually seen in print. However, the editors knew that the finding would probably get leaked to the press before publication unless they fast-tracked it. "A Linkage between DNA Markers on the X Chromosome and Male Sexual Orientation" was submitted on April 2, 1993, accepted on June 17, 1993, and published in July 1993.

When Hamer came to the realization, back in 1991, that doing research on the genetics of sexual orientation would be anything but boring, he had no idea just how interesting things would get. Immediately after the publication of Hamer's findings, the media pounced upon the story. *Time* magazine picked up the story within days of the study's publication.[30] *U.S. News and World Report* ran a story on the same day. The study became fodder for talk shows, political cartoons, and political T-shirts ("Xq28 – Thanks for the genes, Mom!"). To make things even more interesting, Hamer's study was published one day before the deadline for the Pentagon to approve a new Department of Defense policy on homosexuality – the policy that came to be known as "don't ask, don't tell." The timing, although entirely coincidental, was viewed with suspicion – in a *Nightline* interview with Ted Koppel, Hamer was grilled about the timing of the study.[31]

For the most part, however, the media reported

the findings in a "careful and responsible" way, according to Hamer.[32]   Political figures and activists were not necessarily so careful and responsible. For example, one conservative senator was very upset that the National Cancer Institute, in his mind, was diverting resources from cancer research to sexual orientation research. Members of Hamer's research team were subjected to harassment – in one instance, an antigay "psychologist" posed as a reporter and got into the NIH building where Hamer's team conducted their work. He then harassed members of the research team about their personal lives and sexual orientations until one member of the team threw him out. Even some pro-gay activists were upset with the study, fearing that the findings could lead to the genetic manipulation of sexual orientation through gene therapy and abortion of gay fetuses. At the extreme, Hamer was accused of having ties to eugenic ideologies.[33]   While most of his colleagues at the NIH defended his work and his credibility, allegations of scientific misconduct were made against Hamer by one of his colleagues.[34] Like Alfred Kinsey's work half a century earlier, Hamer's findings had clearly touched a cultural nerve.

If Hamer was unprepared for the massive media response to his work, being subpoenaed to testify in court probably threw him completely off-guard. A year earlier, in 1992, Colorado voters approved Amendment 2, an initiative that prohibited the state from giving

homosexuals protected status. Legal challenges to the
initiative were filed immediately after passage, and Hamer
found himself at the vortex of a political firestorm.
Opponents to the initiative seized upon Hamer's findings,
hoping to capitalize on the argument that people who
have a deeply ingrained (or genetic) characteristic should
be entitled to protected status. Despite being grilled
by the assistant district attorney, Hamer's study was
influential in overturning Amendment 2 – in his ruling,
the judge referred to "the preponderance of credible
evidence suggesting that there is a biologic [*sic*] or genetic
'component' of sexual orientation."[35]

At the time, was there really a preponderance
of evidence? We had high concordance rates for
homosexuality from Bailey and Pillard's twin studies.
We had Simon LeVay's research on INAH-3. We had a
few more studies that predated LeVay's work identifying
sexually dimorphic traits. And we had Hamer's Xq28
finding. None of those findings had been replicated –
meaning that none of these studies had been repeated to
see whether or not the initial finding held. Since then, a
multitude of efforts were launched to replicate Hamer's
findings. Although several other analyses of the Xq28
marker have been conducted since 1993 with mixed
results, a meta-analysis (a procedure in which the results
from several studies are combined to produce an overall
measure of treatment effect) of all of these linkage

studies suggests a significant link to Xq28.[36] In addition, a 2005 study conducted by Brian Mustanski and his colleagues found markers on chromosomes 7, 8, and 10 in addition to Xq28.[37] Replication of findings, the final step in the scientific method, closes the circle. From a scientific standpoint, Hamer's objectivity paid off – even if there were personal consequences.

Like most researchers in the "hard sciences," very little about Dean Hamer's personal beliefs or experience, including his sexuality, was reflected in his work. In most cases, this is the expectation – scientists are expected to be objective and unbiased regarding their work. And yet, in the field of LGBT research, most researchers engage in some form of self-disclosure, be it their sexual orientation or their political leanings. Simon LeVay made clear his sexual orientation from the outset. Michael Bailey has pictures of his children and his ex-wife on his Northwestern University website, and he refers to his heterosexual orientation throughout his book, *The Man Who Would Be Queen*. Gregory Herek makes clear his political leanings through his involvement with the legislature and the courts. Hamer, in contrast, is strikingly silent.

As improprietous as this might be, I found myself

wondering if Dean Hamer was gay. It wasn't anything
that he said – it was what went unsaid. Having been
cautious about my own sexual orientation in the past, I'd
learned that the less personal information I volunteered,
the better. Instead of awkwardly avoiding pronouns
when referring to a significant other, it's just easier to
avoid talking about that significant other altogether. If
a political discussion involving homosexuality arose, it
was safer to listen in rather than volunteering an opinion.
Most people probably wouldn't even notice these tactics,
unless you've used them yourself – and as I read more
about Hamer and his work, my suspicions were raised.
No mention was made of a significant other in the
acknowledgements to his book, *The Science of Desire*. In
contrast to Simon LeVay, who was very open about the
fact that his research interests took a U-turn due to a
personal crisis, Hamer's description of his own research
trajectory was very impersonal. Never once did Hamer
reflect on his own personal feelings or political leanings
regarding homosexuality. And interestingly, one of his
research colleagues made what I perceived as a veiled
reference to his sexual orientation as she described herself
as "the only member of the team that was *public* about her
sexual orientation" (emphasis added).[38] I found myself
wanting to know more about this enigmatic researcher.

Why would Dean Hamer conceal his sexuality?
And did he even actively conceal it? Either way, having

never spoken with him, I can only speculate. Hamer took a big risk when he decided to abandon ten years' worth of MT gene transcription research and shift his interest to sexual orientation. Little did he know how much controversy would get stirred up as a result of his work, and little did he know how much his own reputation would be put to the test. I imagine that this was the reason his sexual orientation and political leanings took the back burner – regardless of whether it was a conscious choice to do so. Most scientists who are open about their sexual orientation end up being accused of engaging in "activist research" – biased with a political agenda. Even though Hamer found himself caught in the midst of a fiery controversy, he always presented the image of the objective scientist.

While Hamer was granting television interviews, testifying in court, and generally rising to the level of minor celebrity status, unrest was concealed in the underbelly of the NIH. Much of it centered around a little-known postdoctoral research associate named Angela Pattatucci. Pattatucci was part of Hamer's research team and the last author of the Xq28 study. Hamer was the first author listed in the Xq28 study, and therefore received the most credit for it (and was most visibly represented in the press). Pattatucci, in contrast, was hidden in the invisible "et al." of the research team. Hamer had a doctoral degree from Harvard University and an established tenure at NIH; Pattatucci was a postdoctoral research associate with no job security or career pedigree. Hamer was an older white male whose sexual orientation wasn't made public; Pattatucci was an out Latina lesbian. Hamer was protected to some degree by a wall of privilege – some of it earned, like his body of work at NIH, some of it due to his status as a white male. Pattatucci had no protections whatsoever, and stood the most to lose.

Pattatucci's presence on the research team brought to light at least two major issues – the first being the issue of legitimacy. Hamer had a long history of conducting "hard science," and therefore was viewed as a legitimate researcher. Pattatucci's research interests, which centered mainly around lesbian health issues, were never viewed by the NIH as being a legitimate area of study. For example, there was an offshoot of the original study focusing on lesbians that Pattatucci directed. Hamer's success at securing funding for his study was a cakewalk compared to Pattatucci's efforts. The NIH review committee couldn't see the point of studying lesbian health – or anything having to do with lesbianism, for that matter. As a result, the team never got funding approval, and the research team ended up diverting funds from their own budget to collect data on lesbians. That research still remains unfinished, as Pattatucci left the NIH for reasons to be described below, and no one else took the reins.

It wasn't just about securing funds for lesbian research – it was about the perception of credibility and legitimacy. Pattatucci "was the out Lesbian conducting research on Lesbians – an inauthentic woman conducting inauthentic research. In its best light, my work was cute. I was like the young daughter in 'girl training' that greets her father at the door with the proclamation that she helped cook dinner with mommy. No one believes that she actually contributed to the success of the meal – she's just there and cute."[39]   Hamer was credited with conducting serious science, and Pattatucci's contributions were condescendingly regarded as cute.

Not only was Pattatucci attempting to conduct research on lesbians, she was the only member of the team who was public about her sexual orientation. "I completely underestimated the profound impact of me being an out Lesbian – the only member of the team who was public about her sexual orientation – would have on how the study was perceived," says Pattatucci.[40] Pattatucci's naïveté ended up having serious consequences, signaling the end of her short tenure at NIH. For one thing, Hamer was viewed as a "legitimate scientist" and received the bulk of the positive press regarding their study. Pattatucci, in contrast, was "an activist with an agenda – all because I was an out Lesbian."[41]   While Hamer was granting interviews and rising to the level of minor celebrity status, Pattatucci was ordered by one of her supervisors to say nothing, out of fear over what "their token Latina lesbian might say to the press."[42] While Hamer was testifying in court in efforts to overturn Amendment 2, Pattatucci was being virulently attacked on the U.S. Senate floor by Senator Jesse Helms. While Hamer continued his research on sexual orientation and AIDS, Pattatucci was quietly informed that her employment contract at the NIH would not be renewed.

Obviously, Pattatucci's career suffered as a result of being out and pursuing her research interests. Does that mean that, in the world of the "hard sciences," one must remain closeted and play the game of bureaucracy? Obviously Hamer knew how to play the game – the combination of a solid track record, savvy grant-writing, and a veneer of objectivity were crucial in the success of this study. And clearly, Hamer received the accolades and Pattatucci was a casualty of war.

One wonders, too, if Pattatuci's career was shattered only because she was open about her sexuality, or if being female and having a research interest in lesbians had anything to do with it. Given that, to date, almost all of the studies investigating the causes of homosexuality focus on males, this isn't an out-in-left-field question. Simon LeVay, for example, only examined the brains of gay men. Very few female researchers have broken the glass ceiling within the small LGBT research clique, and almost no mainstream research exists that explores the causes of female homosexuality. If "playing the game" means securing large-scale funding by remaining closeted *and* studying only the dominant gender group, then clearly the rules of the game need to be changed. But watch out – as we'll see in Chapter 5, bringing women into the picture changes the LGBT research landscape significantly, with weighty political consequences.

———

Hamer took a strong U-turn when he abandoned his MT gene transcription work, switching to "gay gene" research. He took another unpredictable U-turn in 2004 when he published *The God Gene*, which details his research on VMAT2, a gene thought to be associated with spirituality. But that same year, his most courageous U-turn took place when his marriage to longtime partner Joe Wilson was made public in *The New York Times*.[43] In 2009, Hamer and Wilson produced the film "Out in the Silence," which chronicles the disapproving reactions of a small town in Pennsylvania to their marriage. Interestingly enough, it was his Xq28 work that paved the way for

Hamer to shift gears from science to filmmaking. On
the "Out in the Silence" promotional website, Hamer's
profile states the following:

> Scientist turned filmmaker Dean Hamer became
> interested in journalism and filmmaking as a result
> of   being a frequent guest on television news
> shows to discuss his research on AIDS, human
> sexuality, and behavior genetics. Convinced
> that there was a better way to communicate the
> complex scientific and social ideas raised by these
> topics, he decided to try his own hand at turning
> these stories into compelling documentaries.[44]

Hamer had produced several other films prior to
"Out in the Silence," most of which had an LGBT focus,
and all of which had been showcased in various film
festivals and won numerous awards. However, the choice
to co-produce a film whose subject matter involved an
intense level of personal disclosure reflects a radical
departure from the impersonality of science. So which
has had the more powerful impact? The Xq28 research,
which created a tidal wave in the media and in the scientific
community, but which required the imprisonment of his
sexual identity? Or his documentary work, which hasn't
been on the radar of the mainstream media, and hasn't
resulted in any waves of state or federal policy change,
but allows room for complete personal authenticity?

4

SUSPICIOUSLY STRAIGHT

People who study sexual orientation are often automatically assumed to be gay themselves. And there is more than a grain of truth in this. Look at Simon LeVay. Or Dean Hamer. Or Gregory Herek, Ritch Savin-Williams, Lisa Diamond. Or 99% of the other scientists documented in this book. The list goes on and on. In fact, it's very difficult to identify any heterosexuals who devote their entire career to the study of homosexuality. Many straight people get uncomfortable in the gay and lesbian section of a bookstore – why on earth would they want to eat, live, and breathe homosexuality? For J. Michael Bailey, it might be because sexual orientation is an inherently interesting – and controversial – topic.

Bailey certainly thrives on controversy, and perhaps he intuitively sensed the level of excitement this area of research would bring. Little did he know.

Like many other scientists who study sexual orientation, including Simon LeVay and Dean Hamer, Bailey embarked on his career as a sex researcher in a fortuitous way. As a graduate student at the University of Texas, Bailey conducted research on the genetic aspects of schizophrenia and IQ. The turning point came when he needed to come up with a dissertation topic – a process which has held up many a graduate student from completing their degree. A dissertation needs to offer a new contribution to the field. It can reveal new findings, it can present a novel theoretical perspective, or it can point future research into a different direction. It needs to be much more than just a review of existing research – and, if he were to stick with the topics of schizophrenia and IQ, it might have been challenging for Bailey to do more than regurgitate old ideas. So Bailey shifted focus and turned his attention to the biology of sexual orientation, specifically looking at what is referred to as the "prenatal stress theory" of homosexuality – the idea that homosexuality is more likely among fetuses who experience stress while in utero. Bailey was also influenced by the work of German scientist Günter Dorner, who had provided support for prenatal stress theory by determining that mothers of gay men born during World War II had much more stressful pregnancies than mothers of heterosexual men during that same time period. Bailey attempted to replicate this finding, using a stronger methodological approach – and found no support whatsoever for prenatal stress theory.[45]

Researchers are often disappointed when their findings are "nonsignificant," at least statistically speaking. Most studies with statistically nonsignificant findings don't get published, and they certainly don't generate headlines. However, sometimes a random finding emerges from the research – something that wasn't the original focus of the study, but has some statistical or practical significance. Bailey, in addition to asking mothers about the level of stress they'd experienced during their pregnancies, had also asked respondents to document relatives' sexual orientations – and found that 20% of the gay men's brothers were also gay (compared to 1% of straight men's brothers).[46] This *very* statistically significant finding launched Bailey's career and defined him as a sexual orientation researcher. It also put him in contact with Richard Pillard, who had documented that homosexuality tends to run in families, and after Bailey earned his doctorate, the two researchers began their collaboration.

Michael Bailey has conducted scores of studies on sexual orientation, on topics ranging from comparisons of sexual arousal between men and women (both heterosexual and homosexual), femininity and gender nonconformity in gay men, and the accuracy of "gay-dar" (that sixth sense that many of us claim to have when determining whether someone is gay or straight).[47] Almost all of his research has been attacked by either the religious right or by gay and lesbian activists, which puts him in good company with other sexual orientation researchers. By far, though, the studies that have been the most attention-grabbing are his twin studies, which assess the heritability of sexual orientation (the degree to which homosexuality runs in families).

In order to understand how twin studies are conducted, it's important to know the difference between monozygotic (identical) and dizygotic (fraternal) twins. Monozygotic twins develop from a single fertilized egg and therefore are identical, genetically speaking, while dizygotic twins develop from two different fertilized eggs, having about the same degree of genetic similarity as non-twin siblings. By comparing sets of monozygotic twins to sets of dizygotic twins (or non-twin siblings), researchers can estimate how much of a particular trait is due to genetics or to environmental effects – attempting to provide clarity to the nature-nurture controversy.

In Bailey and Pillard's twin study, the findings were striking. In the case of male identical twins, if one twin was gay, there was a 52% chance that the other twin would be gay as well. For fraternal twins, there was a 24%

probability, and adoptive brothers had an 11% chance of being gay. Bailey and Pillard later used the same methodology to study lesbian identical twins, fraternal twins, and sisters, and found similar concordance rates.[48]

Fifty-two percent is a high concordance rate, and a noteworthy finding. Schizophrenia, which is considered to be a highly heritable condition, has about a 48% concordance rate. Recent studies of intelligence suggest about a 75% concordance rate, although estimates vary from study to study. Both schizophrenia and intelligence – Bailey's early areas of study – have a well-established genetic basis, and Bailey and Pillard's twin studies introduced the strong possibility of a familial basis to homosexuality.

Bailey has weathered the same critiques that were hurled at Simon LeVay and Dean Hamer for their work. And again, while the response from anti-gay activists was to be expected, the reactions from the gay community were unexpectedly mixed and extreme. Some have wielded his findings to disprove the idea that homosexuality is a choice or an act of defiance against God's will. Others have accused Bailey of pathologizing homosexuality, particularly when Bailey uses phrases like "evolutionarily maladaptive" to describe homosexuality.[49] (When applied to homosexuality, the term "evolutionarily maladaptive," which sounds insulting, really means that homosexuality doesn't facilitate reproduction and survival of the species, at least not in an obvious way.) By far, however, the most derisive accusation fired at Bailey involves his alleged support of homosexual eugenics – the selection of specific genes to ensure heterosexuality and discourage homosexuality.[50] If homosexuality has a genetic basis, and if scientists can identify the specific gene (or combination of genes) involved, then that information could be used to weed homosexuality out of the gene pool. Homosexuality could be added to the repertoire of conditions tested prenatally through amniocentesis, and parents could then make the decision to abort the fetus should it test positive. Or heterosexuality could be ensured by using pre-implantation techniques, such as genetically testing embryos for markers on X or Y chromosomes and then only implanting those embryos without markers for homosexuality.

If this sounds like a bizarre science fiction novel, it's important to be aware that eugenics has been used in ugly, ugly ways in the United States and around the world. Examples include state laws that required the sterilization of the mentally ill and of "imbeciles" (people of low intelligence), immigration laws preventing certain groups from coming into the U.S., anti-miscegenation laws banning interracial marriage, and, ironically enough, Planned Parenthood's fight for the legalization of contraception, which, while championed as a success in the fight for women's reproductive rights, was also intended to prevent poor people from bearing children. While all of these examples seem outrageous and offensive, it's also important to know that these practices were taking place as recently as the 1970s. This is not ancient history we're talking about. And the fight for gay and lesbian rights still has a long way to go.

Unfortunately, Bailey's libertarian stance on homosexual eugenics doesn't endear himself to the gay and lesbian community very well. His opinion stands in stark contrast to that of Dean Hamer, who, in his final comments in the *Science* article documenting the Xq28 finding, broke out of his "objective scientist" persona and made clear his own personal ethics regarding eugenics.[51] Bailey, in contrast, deviates from the gay activist position to the extreme. Although he makes clear that homophobia is not a good reason for parents to select against homosexual children, in several publications he cites other reasons parents might have for taking steps to have a heterosexual child. These reasons include wanting to spare their children from having to deal with homophobia; the wish to maximize their chances of having grandchildren; or wanting to have children who are like themselves, in the sense that they could enter a heterosexual marriage and reproduce heterosexually. In an article published in the *Archives of Sexual Behavior*, Bailey and his colleague Aaron Greenberg provided a lengthy discussion of this issue, which is repeated in abbreviated form in Bailey's book, *The Man Who Would Be Queen*. Bailey and Greenberg generally conclude that selecting for heterosexuality is "morally acceptable" and an example of the parental right to raise children however they wish to raise them. They also argue that, if a person supports the right to have an abortion, then it's illogical to *only* oppose abortion due to homosexuality. Lastly, Bailey and Greenberg point out that most parents make all sorts of attempts to ensure that their children will possess certain characteristics. When a pregnant woman chooses to abstain from alcohol or drugs, for example, or when parents read to their children, they are encouraging the development of certain desired characteristics, such as intelligence. Bailey sees the choice to select for heterosexuality no differently.[52]

No one ever accused Bailey of being a people-pleaser – that's for sure. In fact, Bailey is infamous for placing himself at the vortex of intellectual controversy (as we'll see more starkly later on). Obviously, Bailey's opinions make people very uncomfortable and angry – and this seems to be the thread that is woven through the tapestry of his career. Of course, Bailey isn't suggesting that we institute a nationwide government policy to eradicate homosexuality – he's talking about the freedom to make personal decisions. And yet, do we really have the right to engage in the population control of an oppressed group of people – even if it's just at the level of a personal decision?

Years ago, I saw an episode of *Law and Order* (I'm a big *Law and Order* junkie) where a white woman, after strangely giving birth to a black baby, eventually discovered that her seemingly-white husband had concealed the fact that his own father was African-American. What if this woman had found out during her pregnancy that her baby was black – would it have been ethical for her to abort the baby? She may want her child to be like her, or she may wish to shield her child from racism. Are these acceptable reasons for aborting that child? Or we could use the example of Down syndrome – a condition that is associated with various health issues, but isn't a fatal condition. Prenatal screening for Down syndrome has become routine, and over 90% of identified Down syndrome pregnancies are terminated.[53] Is this ethical?

Some would argue that science-fiction-style eugenics is already taking place, and that lesbian couples, ironically enough, are unwittingly at the epicenter. Many lesbian couples (and heterosexual couples with fertility issues) utilize sperm banks, which all have selection criteria for their donors. Some of these sperm banks have more stringent criteria than others. For example, California Cryobank, one of the most widely used sperm banks, only accepts about 1% of donor applicants. Donors must be enrolled in or possess a degree from a major four-year university. They are also required to be young (between 19 and 34 years old), at least 5'9", slender, and free of genetic conditions.[54] Other sperm banks have less rigorous standards, but they still require certain things of their donors. And after the sperm banks select their donors, prospective parents undertake their own selection process. If parents decided to select a heterosexual donor rather than a gay donor, would that be unethical? In reality, this is unlikely to happen – all sperm banks, per a 2005 Food and Drug Administration regulation, require that an anonymous sperm donor must not have engaged in homosexual sex for five years.[55] The FDA asserts that gay men possess a higher-than-average risk of carrying the AIDS virus, and this accounts for the ban. However, if homosexuality is a predominantly genetically-based phenomenon, the ban would effectively weed out homosexuality from the sperm bank gene pool.

In his book, *The Man Who Would Be Queen*, Bailey ends this discussion with the following comments – probably as a way of putting the eugenics debate into perspective:

> The belief that studying the causes of homosexuality will eventually harm gay people is a highly speculative one. There is no good reason to dislike or desire to harm gay

people, and so it is difficult to argue that good scientific studies or rational, open discussion will have that end. In fact, I think that the more we know about homosexuality, the better attitudes toward gay people will become.

Every day gay people suffer real harm – indignities and abuse committed by those with irrational prejudice. We can do a lot more good by focusing on this problem, and trying to solve it, than by speculating about the harm that science might cause.[56]

Bailey makes an excellent – and critical – point. And yet, although Bailey has said and written many things that have commanded the attention of gay and lesbian activists, this was not one of them – even though Bailey's statements clearly speak against the injustice of homophobia. Why is there so much suspicion of Bailey's motives? Is it because he's straight? Is it because he's not interested in furthering any political agenda on behalf of gay and lesbian people – or anybody else? Most other researchers who study gay and lesbian issues are also involved in the gay rights effort in some way. Not Bailey. In fact, Bailey sees the politicization of "gay science" as an irritation and a hindrance to scientific progress.[57]

And yet, science influences politics, whether we like it or not. Hopefully, the more positive attitudes towards homosexuality become, the more ridiculous the concept of aborting a gay fetus, or rejecting sperm that might yield a gay child, or discarding an embryo that carries the "gay gene." We can only hope. In any case, as we'll see later in this book, the controversy regarding the search for the causes of homosexuality – and the antipathy towards Michael Bailey – only gets more heated from here.

5

SWINGING BOTH WAYS

com•ing-out (kŭm ĭng-out') also **coming out**
n.
1. A social debut.
2. A revelation or acknowledgment that one is a gay man,
a lesbian, or a bisexual.[58]

*When I joined the Navy, I had a strong feeling that I was gay. I
had been attracted to men all my life, but being raised in a small
town in Kentucky in the 50's and 60's, well, we just didn't talk
about such things.*

I married (a Mormon man) at 19 like any good Mormon girl

would. I had hoped all I needed was just to be "loved right." At the time I tried not to entertain the thought of anything relating to being gay.

I've known for years that I'm a lesbian, although people who've known me for a long time fail to believe this because I used to feel like I had to pretend to be straight so that people wouldn't find me out.

As time went by, and I plunged more into adolescence, I got a clearer picture of who I was. And I wasn't sure I liked it. I was confused, and frightened by what I felt; but also couldn't stop it. Finally the word for it entered my head, and I knew what it meant, and what people thought about it. One day, while alone in my house, I was lying on my bed. I said out loud to myself, "You're gay."

The stories are endless. They vary only in the details, but the narrative framework tends to be the same. He has a secret, hidden away, waiting to be revealed. It might be exposed in adolescence, or early adulthood. In some cases the truth remains hidden for years, maybe decades. In the meantime, he may perform the heterosexual charade, in the hopes that play-acting will become reality. He may fall into the depths of depression and isolation, or alcohol and drug use, or other self-destructive behaviors. Or he may appear to have the perfect life – a wife, children, a good job, respected standing in the community. But eventually the truth breaks free – abandoning his former life, he makes his debut into the world.

This is the typical "coming-out" narrative, based on the assumption that a homosexual identity is hidden, just waiting to be unearthed. While the details vary, the storyboard retains the same format – the epiphany, the inner turmoil, the secret double-life, the first disclosures, the vow to live authentically. For three decades, from *The Original Coming-Out Stories* to the reality show *Coming Out Stories*, we've come to expect a linear, predictable process. And it all began with a theory developed by a then-little-known psychologist by the name of Vivienne Cass.

Most academic psychologists are workhorses. They are painstaking in their research efforts, often studying the same concept throughout their entire career. They work tirelessly to publish their work in top-tier journals. They teach undergraduate and graduate-level courses. Those who are trained as clinicians provide countless hours of psychotherapy. A lucky few strike gold, publishing a paper that becomes a classic in the field. Even fewer get on the map for their political and activist efforts. Within five years of earning her master's degree in psychology, Vivienne Cass did both.

In the 1970s, Cass was a young, newly-minted therapist in Western Australia. While she was in the process of earning her master's degree, she established

the Homosexual Counselling and Information Service of
Western Australia (now known as the Gay and Lesbian
Community Services of Western Australia). This was
1974 – five years after Stonewall, and a time where gay and
lesbian-oriented services were practically nonexistent. To
put this into perspective, the Homosexual Counselling
and Information Service was the first GLBT center to be
established *in the entire southern half of the planet.* And this
was done by a twenty-something student – before she
had finished her master's degree. Clearly, Cass was a go-
getter – and her accomplishments didn't stop there. Five
years after she founded her counseling service (and four
years after earning her master's degree), Cass published
in the *Journal of Homosexuality* her now-classic paper,
"Homosexual Identity Formation: A Theoretical Model"
– the paper that anchored the way we understand coming
out and homosexual identity development.[59]

So how does Cass provide the theoretical
groundwork for the typical coming-out story? It all starts
with "coming out to oneself." When it first dawns on
the individual that he or she might be gay, lesbian, or
bisexual, the person has entered what Cass refers to as
the *identity confusion* stage. Denial, confusion, and distress
are common reactions. In some cases, the individual may
refuse to further consider the possibility of being gay –
this is referred to as *identity foreclosure.* The most extreme
form of identity foreclosure is suicide. However, most

people continue to grapple with the very real possibility that they might be gay, which helps them to transition to the next stage. This process may vary from person to person depending on their individual values, beliefs about homosexuality, and support from people such as family and friends.

According to Cass, the transition from awareness to acceptance of the possibility that the individual might be gay, lesbian, or bisexual marks the beginning of *identity comparison*. This is the first point in the process where the individual may be committing, albeit tentatively, to a non-heterosexual identity. In this stage, the individual may begin to feel dissonance between their earlier heterosexual identity and their current self-perception. This stage is potentially marked by a sense of isolation, grief, and fear.

As acceptance for a non-heterosexual identity increases, the individual moves from identity comparison to *identity tolerance*. Instead of thinking, "I might be gay," the individual shifts to "I'm probably gay." At this point, the individual may begin to seek contact with members of the LGB community. This is the stage where individuals may feel as if they're living a double life – presenting a heterosexual image to their families, friends, and the larger society, while exploring their sexual orientation through seeking contact with members of the LGB community. Knowledge of lesbian, gay and bisexual people may be based more on stereotypes than on reality, and the individual may try on their non-heterosexual identity by experimenting with stereotypical roles.

The process of coming out typically begins in the *identity acceptance* stage. In this stage, the individual has come to accept him or herself as lesbian, gay, or bisexual, and is now addressing the issue of self-disclosure to others. In addition, the individual continues to involve him or herself with the gay and lesbian community.

Coming out is no easy task. Many gay and lesbian people choose to come out to the "safest" person first. For some people, that might be through an anonymous contact on the Internet; for others, it might be a face-to-face disclosure with another gay person; for still others, a close and accepting friend might be the first to receive the information. Many individuals dread coming out to their parents, fearing rejection, disappointment, anger, and abandonment. Those who are preparing to come out to their spouses or to their children might be bracing themselves even more strongly. And yet, coming out is a milestone of the gay and lesbian experience. Everyone remembers their coming-out stories vividly, especially when it involves the people we're closest to.

Coming out marks a shift towards authenticity. Something very powerful happens when we align our private self with our public image. At the same time, living authentically means letting go of heterosexual privilege, and becoming more aware of homophobia. Holding hands with a lover in public might not be a safe option anymore. Bringing a significant other home to meet Mom and Dad could be more stressful than it would ordinarily be – and in some cases it might not even happen. Old friends might slowly drop out of our lives. Going to church, which might have been fulfilling at one time, might be stressful and upsetting, depending on the church's preachings regarding homosexuality. In one survey of gay and lesbian youth, as a result of coming out, 60% experienced some verbal or physical harassment from family, 36% experienced verbal insults, and 10% experienced physical assaults.[60] Being out, particularly for gay men, increases the likelihood of being a victim of a hate crime.[61] Moreover, many states don't have civil rights laws prohibiting discrimination based on sexual orientation, so being out could potentially result in legally-sanctioned housing and employment discrimination. The more we present ourselves authentically, the more sexual oppression becomes visible on the radar screen.

A very legitimate reaction to these injustices is anger, and anger is the benchmark of the *identity pride* stage. Most of this anger is directed towards heterosexuals and mainstream society as a whole. The world becomes split into "gay" (good) and "straight" (bad), and the individual immerses him or herself within the haven of the gay and lesbian community. While some people foreclose at this stage, others progress to *identity synthesis*. In this stage, the individual shifts from viewing themselves completely in terms of their gayness or lesbianism, towards a more integrated sense of self. At this point, sexual orientation is just one aspect of their identity, and the individual develops a more holistic view of who they are.

During a time when a homosexual identity was far more stigmatized than it is today, Cass's model provided a beacon of hope for lesbians and gay men who were struggling with accepting their sexual orientation. Gathering information about sexual orientation from books, magazines, and websites (in this day and age); seeking contact with the lesbian and gay community through social gatherings and support groups; coming out to others; and becoming politically active – all of these activities pave the way towards self-acceptance. None of this can happen without a cohesive, strong, and supportive lesbian and gay community – at least not easily. Because of that, Cass's model has likely contributed to the massive growth of the "gay and lesbian community" – Gay Pride celebrations, LGBT resource and community centers, gay-supportive therapists (who can help people weather the storm of the early stages of identity development), lesbian and gay bookstores, websites focused on LGBT issues, LGBT-friendly sex shops, LGBT-themed concerts, vacations, cruises – you name it. Community fosters identity.

Although Cass's model has weathered numerous criticisms over the years, the spirit of her model has persisted. In fact, it's probably fair to say that her model has unilaterally dictated the way we think about gay and lesbian identity formation. Yet a number of researchers have attempted to improve upon the model, for various reasons. For example, Eli Coleman's model establishes the coming-out process as the locus of his theory. His stages progress as follows:

- *Pre-coming out*, in which initial awareness of same-sex attraction rises to the surface, resulting in a range of emotional reactions;

- *Coming out*, where acceptance of one's homosexuality begins to take hold, and first disclosures take place;

- *Exploration*, a quasi-adolescent stage which is characterized by sexual and social experimentation in relationships;

- *First relationship*, marked by the desire to move from experimentation to deeper and more intimate relationships, and by the development of relationship skills; and

- *Integration*, in which, like Cass's identity synthesis stage, the individual moves towards self-actualization, reconciling their public and private selves and living more confidently and authentically.[62]

Several years later, in 1989, Richard Troiden, a sociologist, introduced the notion of age-specific stages and transitions. His model includes the following four stages:

• *Sensitization*, occurring before puberty, in which heterosexuality is unquestioningly assumed, despite the fact that the individual may be displaying gender nonconformity;

• *Identity confusion*, the stage of adolescence, where the possibility of homosexuality is considered, resulting in inner turmoil and uncertainty;

• *Identity assumption*, in which the individual claims a homosexual identity, and contacts with other gay and lesbian people are made; and

• *Commitment*, in which homosexuality is accepted as a way of life.[63]

Other models exist as well. For example, Ruth Fassinger developed a four-stage model that addresses both individual sexual identity development and group membership identity development, both of which include an awareness phase, an exploration phase, a deepening and commitment phase, and an internalization/synthesis phase.[64] Anthony D'Augelli broadens the model to encompass several aspects of identity, including intimacy status, identity as a gay son or lesbian daughter, and involvement in the gay and lesbian community.[65] And yet, all of these models, although packaged differently, are strikingly similar. In fact, if I were a student memorizing these stage models for a test, I think I'd have a hard time keeping them straight (no pun intended). They all retain the "typical coming-out narrative," but they are packaged differently. All of them assume that there is a beginning and an end to the sexual identity development process, and that the process unfolds in a linear fashion. None of them incorporate bisexual identities (although some models just add the word "bisexual" without changing the model to reflect their experiences). In fact, Cass had initially considered bisexuality to be a form of identity foreclosure, although she later reversed her position and came to view bisexuality as a distinct orientation. Probably the most glaring issue with these models is that they reinforce the notion that each person's sexual orientation is fixed and immutable, just waiting to be discovered, accepted, and integrated into the rest of our identity. The reality is that this just isn't always true.

Activists in the gay and lesbian community don't like to hear this, which in some ways is understandable. A growing body of evidence – concordance rates, INAH-3, Xq28 – suggests a strong biological basis to sexual orientation. Gay rights activists are highly invested in the idea that sexual orientation is a function of biology (rather than a choice), for it is a powerful argument for legal protections against discrimination. And since the 1960s, coming out has been viewed not only as a personal journey towards authenticity, but as a political strategy to counter sexual prejudice.

If there is a counter-narrative to the typical coming-out story, my friend Shannon's story is an excellent example.[66] For years she had identified unambiguously as a lesbian – she was active in lesbian social groups, political organizations, and a gay and lesbian-affirming spiritual community. She was also in a long-term relationship with a woman – until she met Anton, a heterosexual man whom she met through her spiritual activities. Over time, her attraction to him became more and more difficult to deny, and she eventually made the painful decision to leave her partner and marry Anton. Although she knew she was being true to herself by making that decision, she underestimated the powerfully negative and angry reaction she received from her lesbian friends. Friends she'd known for years refused to speak with her anymore. The spiritual community that had once been so welcoming of her became hostile territory. In fact, this second coming-out experience was significantly more difficult, painful, and traumatic than her coming-out as a lesbian. Instead of celebrating her authenticity, her once-supportive lesbian community viewed her as a traitor. Acknowledging her attraction to men defied the conventional wisdom of the traditional lesbian identity development narrative.

Shannon's experience reflects an emerging counter-narrative to the typical coming-out story, and the scripter of this narrative is a young researcher named Lisa Diamond. Diamond, a developmental psychologist at the University of Utah, has studied the development of sexual orientation in women for the past ten years, beginning when she was a graduate student at Cornell University. Like Vivienne Cass, Diamond broke the mold very early on in her career. As early as 1997 (shortly after she earned her master's degree), she utilized the term "sexual fluidity" to describe the trajectories of sexual identity development in women.[67] Sexual fluidity, according to Diamond, refers to "situationally-dependent flexibility in women's sexual responsiveness":

> In other words, though women – like men – appear to be born with distinct sexual orientations, these orientations do not provide the last word on their sexual attractions and experiences. Instead, women of all orientations may experience variation in their erotic and affectional feelings as they encounter different situations, relationships, and life stages.[68]

Sexual fluidity reflects the experience of Anne

Heche, who fell in love with Ellen DeGeneres after an exclusively heterosexual past, and who married a man after her relationship with DeGeneres ended. Or Ani DiFranco, a self-avowed bisexual, whose marriage to a man in 1998 was seen as a flagrant betrayal to her lesbian-feminist audiences. Instead of labeling these experiences as "outliers" – which researchers and statisticians often exclude from their analyses because they fall so radically outside the norm – Diamond wondered whether their experiences actually *represented* the norm. Maybe these women don't mess up the bell curve – maybe they *are* the bell curve! She thought about the distinction, for example, between "born" lesbians and "political" lesbians – women who choose lesbianism as an expression of radical feminism. She wanted to better understand the development of bisexual women, who have historically been excluded from sexual orientation research because they "mess up" the theory that sexual orientation is fixed and biologically based. Most importantly, Diamond was fascinated by the notion that female sexuality might not involve stability and continuity over time, and wanted to explore this further.

Diamond conducted what is referred to as a longitudinal study – a study in which a group of participants is followed for an extended period of time. A longitudinal research design is the perfect approach to studying sexual fluidity, for it allows the researcher to study fluctuations in sexual attraction and behavior over time. These are not easy studies to conduct – for one thing, they tend to be quite expensive. It's also difficult to retain the original participant pool – participants may decide that they don't want to take part in the study any longer, or they move and fail to contact the researcher, or they die. Despite the fact that Diamond had no funding sources when she initiated this research, 88% of her original sample remained in the study at the ten-year follow-up – an inconceivable retention rate for longitudinal research.[69]

In order to recruit a sample of participants, Diamond was willing to roll up her sleeves and get her hands dirty. She bought a used car and road-tripped all over New York State. She set up booths at LGBT community events and talked to people about her research. She attended college classes on gender and sexuality. She met with LGBT youth groups and college organizations. Her hard work eventually resulted in a sample of eighty-nine sexual minority women – a decidedly non-representative sample, Diamond admits, for the vast majority were white, college-educated, and middle class. At the beginning of the study, 43% identified as lesbian, 30% labeled themselves as bisexual, and 27% didn't claim a particular label, although they were non-heterosexual. Shortly after the first wave of interviews, Diamond added 11 heterosexual women to the sample.[70]

Five sets of interviews were conducted over a 10-year period – the first were face-to-face, and all subsequent interviews were over the phone. Diamond asked a wide range of questions. She wanted to know what the women experienced when they started questioning their sexuality. She asked participants to share their early memories of sexual feelings and behaviors, as well as their patterns of attractions, friendships, and intimate relationships over time. She asked participants to clarify their current identity, and to rate themselves on a scale from 0-100 regarding their sexual attractions (0=exclusively opposite-sex attractions, 50=equal same-sex and opposite-sex attractions, 100=exclusively same-sex attractions). She also asked participants to report the total number of men and women they'd had sexual contact with – a question that most people would never dream of asking, particularly in an interview format, but that was crucial to this study.[71]

Sexual fluidity was apparent even at the first interview. Half of the lesbian women reported initially coming out as bisexual; one-third of bisexual women said that they had initially come out as lesbian. At the two-year follow-up, one-third of the sample had changed identities, mostly switching from an unlabeled status to lesbian or bisexual. At the third interview, 25% of the women had switched identities, the changes occurring in all directions. One-third of the women made a switch by the fourth interview, and by the fifth interview, another one-third of the women switched. The interesting thing is that this wasn't the same subset of women changing identities – most of the changes were one-time transitions. In fact, the smallest and most atypical group was the women who kept the same identity during the entire 10-year span![72]

Diamond's research turned the fixed-and-unchangeable view of sexual orientation on its head. Granted, much of the supporting evidence for that theory – INAH-3 and Xq28, for example – was generated from studies focusing exclusively on men. Although a few researchers have studied a possible biological basis for female sexual orientation, those studies rarely make headlines – largely because the findings tend to be equivocal. Studies of lesbian twins, for example, haven't consistently yielded high concordance rates for homosexuality. Dean Hamer's search for an X-linked marker in lesbians hit a dead end. Frankly, if these findings did make headlines, modifying the biological basis theory would likely make gay activists very, very nervous. And yet, when we shift the focus from men to women, and from a binary categorization to a more fluid perspective, the data paint a very different picture. Accepting sexual fluidity as a reality means that (1) we have to talk about bisexuality, and (2) we need to address the issue of choice and sexual orientation.

———

Bisexuality is viewed with suspicion. Often it is ignored entirely by researchers. In fact, when I was a graduate student studying body image and internalized homophobia in lesbians, my dissertation committee members strongly advised me to exclude bisexual women from my sample, as they would "complicate" the findings. Bisexuals complicate things. They don't fit into our nice-and-neat categories of gay and straight. They don't always jump on board with the gay and lesbian political agenda – for example, those who practice polyamory throw a political wrench in the argument for same-sex marriage. And so they are excluded, marginalized, trivialized, exoticized – both by mainstream heterosexual culture and by the gay and lesbian community. Bisexuals are scary. They are a threat to the social order. And when we feel threatened, the immature defense of denial can provide relief.

Denial can take many forms. The most basic form of denial is invisibility. It's common to assume that two female lovers are lesbian, or that two male lovers are gay, or that a male and a female are heterosexual – when in fact any or all of them could be bisexual. It's common to expect bisexuals to identify as heterosexual when coupled with the opposite sex, and to identify as gay or lesbian when coupled with the same sex. Of course, the reality is that bisexuals usually look neatly heterosexual or homosexual, depending on whom they're coupled with. We're comfortable with bisexuals until they make themselves visible – and once that happens, a more primitive form of denial might kick in. We cheapen bisexuality by suggesting that bisexuals just haven't made up their minds – they're going through a phase, they're confused, they're a fence-sitter, a switch hitter. We view bisexuality as "trendy," another form of minimization and denial that suggests that bisexuality isn't a "real" sexual orientation.

As if denying one's very existence isn't bad enough, bisexuals are viewed as untrustworthy, dangerous, and sexually insatiable. Recall Sharon Stone's character in *Basic Instinct*, the ice pick-wielding bisexual serial killer. In the classic image of her interrogation, she defiantly smokes a cigarette and crosses and uncrosses her legs, revealing the fact that she isn't wearing any underwear. She has passionate, torrid, violent sex with multiple partners – a male rock star, her female lover, a male police detective. And everyone she has sex with happens to turn up dead (or, in the case of Michael Douglas' character, impending murder is left up to the imagination in a cliffhanger). Bisexuals are viewed as untrustworthy – they could turn on you at any time, never being able to commit to a relationship – or to an identity, for that matter. They spread the AIDS virus by secretly having sex outside of their relationship and transmitting it to their partners. They play both sides of the field so they can take advantage of heterosexual privilege while engaging in same-sex relationships. They're seen as a sex toy, a fetish – someone who is insatiable, always available, wanting to fulfill any radical or kinky sexual fantasy. Bisexuals are dangerous.

All of these stereotypes are examples of biphobia, which, similar to homophobia, technically refers to an irrational fear of and aversion towards bisexual people and bisexuality in general. However, while lesbians and gay men have created a haven for themselves to protect against the effects of homophobia, there is no such haven for bisexuals. Bisexuals get it from both directions – heterosexuals and homosexuals feel threatened by bisexuality, and they attempt to control their fear and anxiety through biphobia. Biphobia allows us to maintain those nice, neat binary categories of straight and gay, reinforcing denial and invisibility. As Robyn Ochs puts it, biphobia allows the "in-group" (whether it's mainstream heterosexual culture or the lesbian and gay community) to mask their insecurities by targeting the "other" as inferior. It enables the in-group to band together against a common enemy, strengthening the group's sense of cohesion.[73]

So, in order to move beyond biphobia, we have to accept the reality of bisexuality. And it is a reality. According to Alfred Kinsey, 46% of males surveyed had experienced both heterosexual and same-sex attractions and behaviors.[74] More recently, a 2002 survey conducted by the National Center for Health Statistics found that 2.8 percent of women ages 18–44 considered themselves bisexual, 1.3 percent homosexual, and 3.8 percent as "something else." Among men, 1.8 percent of men ages 18–44 considered themselves bisexual, 2.3 percent homosexual, and 3.9 percent as "something else."[75] Of course, bisexuality may be more common than the statistics indicate, given that some people may feel more comfortable identifying as "something else" rather than labeling themselves as bisexual. Even so, it's clear that bisexuality exists, and that it is not a rare exception in the queer community.

Moving beyond biphobia also requires that we acknowledge the diversity inherent in bisexuality. Bisexuality (and sexual fluidity) can have many different faces. As an illustration, Ritch Savin-Williams (who, interestingly, was Lisa Diamond's dissertation advisor and mentor at Cornell University), for better or worse, has attempted to shed light on the broad diversity of bisexual identities by creating a nine-item (albeit informal and unsubstantiated) "bisexual typology," which includes the following:

• A "situational" bisexual engages in same-sex behavior due to lack of access to opposite-sex partners, such as in prison.

• A "chic" bisexual is probably heterosexual, but engages in same-sex behavior for social acceptance.

• A "transitional" bisexual uses bisexuality as a bridge to change from one identity to another.

• A "historic" bisexual has engaged in sexual behaviors and fantasies that contradict her current identification.

• A "sequential" bisexual has consecutive relationships with different genders over time.

• A "concurrent" bisexual maintains relationships with both genders at the same time.

• An "experimental" bisexual tests the waters with relationships with both genders to see which gender most appeals to them.

• A "technical" bisexual has sex with both genders but prefer to be called lesbian or gay.

• A "cop-out" bisexual wants the best of both worlds without having to commit to a particular partner, lifestyle, identity, or community.[76]

Whether Savin-Williams' "bisexual subtypes" are accurate, or whether the assigning of labels marginalizes, cheapens, and pathologizes the true bisexual experience, is a question that is certainly up for debate. (Note, of course, that these subtypes were not derived from careful research study.) Putting that issue aside, it's clear that there are many ways to express bisexuality – and some people who fit into these categories may not necessarily label themselves as bisexual. In fact, several of these categories illustrate very clearly the concept of sexual fluidity. And when we examine the languaging used to clarify these subtypes, the uncomfortable notion of – you guessed it – *choice* – emerges. Is a "chic" bisexual *choosing* same-sex behavior for social acceptance? If an "experimental" bisexual is testing the waters, isn't that individual *choosing* to engage in a behavior in order to make sense of his or her identity? If a "transitional" bisexual is changing from one identity to another (a classic example of sexual fluidity), how do we justify the "biologically fixed and immutable" theory of sexual orientation? This is the very issue that has turned the scientific study of sexual orientation on its axis.

Of course, the word "choice" isn't explicitly used in this typology, and few people – even bisexuals – would ever suggest that they "chose" their sexual orientation. The one group within the LGBT community that would clearly define their sexual and relationship practices as

being based on "choice" are the "political lesbians" –
radical lesbian feminists who choose relationships with
women as an expression of feminism and a woman-
oriented culture, and as an action against patriarchy.
Engaging in heterosexual relationships, according to
radical lesbian feminists, is akin to sleeping with the
enemy. Political lesbians don't believe for a second that
sexual orientation is inborn – they state quite openly
that they made a conscious choice to engage in intimate
relationships with women. They don't necessarily view
themselves as having a sexually fluid orientation – in
fact, in their eyes, orientation is irrelevant. It's the
political *choices* that they make that define them. And
this perspective was probably music to the ears of the
religious conservatives, reinforcing the idea that we can
choose to behave in a morally responsible way.

———

   When Diamond's research was initially published
in *Developmental Psychology* in 2000, as anticipated, there
were reverberations throughout the scientific, religious,
and political arenas. Diamond knew from the get-go
that her work might be misinterpreted and misused by
antigay activists. As noted in Chapter 2, people with
pro-gay attitudes tend to believe that sexual orientation
is biologically hard-wired, whereas those with anti-

gay attitudes tend to believe that homosexuality is a
choice.[77] Of course, "choice" is the operative word
here, and it's the issue that the antigay activists seized
upon. Diamond's work was literally hijacked by antigay
activists and organizations, rippling through the print
media, television, and the Internet. Focus on the Family,
Exodus International, and the Family Research Council
– all organizations which condemn homosexuality as
a sin – cited Diamond's work in support of reparative
therapy of homosexuality. However, the most blatant
misrepresentation and misuse of Diamond's work has
been committed by the National Association for Research
and Therapy of Homosexuality (NARTH).

As mentioned earlier, NARTH, according to
its website, "is a professional, scientific organization
that offers hope to those who struggle with unwanted
homosexuality."[78] NARTH takes the position that sexual
orientation change is possible, and that everyone with
unwanted same-sex attractions has a right to receive
reparative therapy. They also take the position that schools
should not present homosexuality as an acceptable
lifestyle, that traditional heterosexual marriage is the ideal
family form and fosters a child's healthy development,
and that homosexuality is against human nature.
However, much of the research they cite in support of
these positions has been conducted by scientists who are
members of NARTH; because of that, it's very difficult

to view their findings as objective and unbiased. To gain credibility, NARTH needed research that was conducted by someone on "the other side," and Lisa Diamond certainly fit the bill. She did her graduate work under the tutelage of Ritch Savin-Williams, a solidly established LGBT researcher at Cornell. She is a long-time member of Division 44 (Society for the Psychological Study of Lesbian, Gay, Bisexual, and Transgender Issues) of the American Psychological Association. And she is out about her own sexual orientation. Lisa Diamond's work was essentially a golden opportunity served up on a silver platter.

Diamond's work has been heavily, heavily utilized by NARTH. For example, in NARTH's fact sheet, "Female Homosexual Development," her research was used as scientific support for a pathological view of lesbianism and bisexuality in women.[79] Christopher Rosik, a clinical psychologist who is also a member of NARTH, has used her work to make a case for reparative therapy; most of his work has been published in professional journals aimed at clergy members and other spiritual advisors, such as the *Journal of Pastoral Care* and the *Journal of Psychology and Theology*.[80] Dean Byrd, a clinical psychologist, current president of NARTH, and author of *Homosexuality and the Church of Jesus Christ* (who also, like Diamond, teaches at the University of Utah), has cited her research in scores of articles on the "homosexuality-as-choice" theory and on conversion therapy.[81]   Her work has even made it into the courts – Dr. Jeffrey Satinover, a psychoanalytically-trained psychiatrist associated with the ex-gay movement, quoted Diamond directly in his 2003 testimony to the Massachusetts Senate Committee Studying Gay Marriage, attempting to refute the claim that "homosexuality is an immutable state of an individual."[82] The quote he used? "Sexual identity is far from fixed in women who aren't exclusively heterosexual."[83] How ironic that her research has been embraced by LGBT researchers, and at the same time Diamond has become the unwilling love-child of the antigay movement.

Diamond has taken both a proactive and reactive approach to the antigay movement's tactics. In her book, anticipating that her work could potentially be misinterpreted or misused, Diamond makes clear that fluidity does not mean that sexual orientation is a matter of choice, that it is caused purely by environmental factors, or that sexual orientation can be changed. According to Diamond, women do in fact have a sexual orientation, but to varying degrees they also possess a capacity for fluidity that is dependent on environmental and situational factors.[84]   Although this might sound as if Diamond is straddling both sides of the fence, her theory is an example of the resolution the psychological community has come to regarding the nature-nurture conflict. Instead of being a question of either-or, psychologists suggest that many behaviors involve *both*; while a biological or genetic predisposition exists, behaviors or characteristics might be triggered by life events or other environmental factors. This general theory – also known as the diathesis-stress model – has been applied to many different issues, including schizophrenia, a psychiatric disorder that has a well-substantiated biological basis. People don't *choose* to become schizophrenic; rather, they possess a biological or genetic vulnerability that interacts with the environment and life events, triggering the disorder. Sexual orientation, while certainly not a disorder or disease, may develop in a similar fashion. Of course, when we're dealing with such an emotionally charged issue, it's far easier to embrace a simplistic, clear-cut explanation, with no ambiguities or complexities. Vivienne Cass's identity formation model is clear-cut, predictable, and unambiguous. The concept of sexual fluidity is not.

Despite her efforts, Diamond's proactive approach did little to curtail the antigay activists' misuse of her work, and at times she has responded to this misuse angrily and reactively. In some ways, this is understandable – given that Diamond hoped to provide validation to the many women who felt their experiences fell outside the norm, her research ended up being used as scientific support for reparative therapy and for the prohibition of gay marriage. Joseph Nicolosi, a co-founder and past president of NARTH, is one of the more vocal individuals to distort Diamond's work. Diamond became aware of the misuse of her work through an organization called TruthWinsOut, which, according to its website, "defends the GLBT community against anti-gay misinformation campaigns, counters the so-called 'ex-gay' industry and educates America about gay life."[85] Addressing Nicolosi directly in a video filmed by TruthWinsOut, an angry Diamond made the following statement: "Dr. Nicolosi, you know exactly what you are doing. This is a willful misuse and distortion of my research. Not an academic disagreement. Not a slight shading of the truth. It's willful distortion. And, it's illegitimate and it's irresponsible and you know that. And you should stop."[86]

So will this stop? Until we can have a more complex and nuanced conversation about sexual orientation, probably not. We have the two sides, with battle lines clearly drawn. One side fears death by discrimination; the other side fears death by sin or immorality. Fear and emotionality often leads to all-or-nothing thinking – either you're born gay, or you choose to be gay. Either homosexuality is biologically hard-wired and immutable, or it can be changed. And the likely reality is this: regardless of whether it's fixed or fluid, our orientation is probably not a choice. How we express that orientation, however, is very much a choice. A man who is attracted to other men can choose to ignore those attractions, marry a woman, and live a heterosexual-looking lifestyle. Unfortunately, if we don't acknowledge our true heart's desires, we are more likely to act them out – often in a destructive manner. As Shannon, the woman described earlier in this chapter, put it, "The wisdom of who we are is going to find a way out." Even if who we are changes over time.

PART II

THE GENDER STORY

6

GOING OFF-MESSAGE

Terminology is everything. The terms we use betray our political leanings and our value systems. When someone refers to a gay person as a "homosexual," for example, their choice of such an antiquated term reveals their ignorance and discomfort. And yet, in the gay and lesbian community, there isn't a generally agreed-upon nomenclature. Different people utilize different terms, and the variety of terms used suggests anything but unity within the gay and lesbian community.

For one thing, non-heterosexual people tend to get offended when they don't feel included. A fair issue, since homosexuality has been silenced, marginalized, and rendered invisible. Some people feel that the word "gay" is all-encompassing; others get offended because they believe that the sole use of the word "gay" is non-inclusive. The spirit of inclusiveness has unfortunately resulted in a multitude of unwieldy alphabet soup abbreviations, the most extensive being LGBTQQIA (lesbian, gay, bisexual, transgender, queer, questioning, intersex, ally). Most people, however, tend to limit their use of initials to four or five, most commonly GLBT or LGBT (sometimes with a Q at the end). Sometimes people get angry about how the initials are positioned – if the "L" comes second, is that a subtle reference to the second-class status women (and lesbians) have historically experienced? And, of course, there's that T, hanging on at the end as an afterthought, or a reluctant concession. And when it comes to transgender identities, the significance of terminology becomes arrestingly clear.

Some terms are fairly universally agreed-upon. *Transgender* is an umbrella term for people whose gender identity, expression or behavior is different from those typically associated with their assigned sex at birth. *Transsexual*, a more specific term, applies to people whose gender identity is different from their assigned sex at birth. Often transsexual people alter or wish to alter their bodies through hormones or surgery in order to make it match their gender identity. Some people, referred to as *cross-dressers* (or *transvestites*, although this is now seen as a derogatory term) dress in clothing traditionally or stereotypically worn by the other sex, but who generally have no intent to live full-time as the other gender. *Drag kings* and *drag queens* are women and men who cross-dress (often as a celebrity) for entertainment purposes at bars, clubs, or other events.

When we move beyond these terms, things get politically murky. In the transgender community, a man who transitions to living as a woman is known as a *male-to-female transsexual* (MTF or M2F); a woman who transitions to living as a man is a *female-to-male transsexual* (FTM or F2M). Increasingly, the trans community prefers the terms *transwoman* and *transman* – transpeople who identify as female or male, respectively. To make things even more complicated, transpeople have a sexual orientation, too – so a transwoman can be heterosexual or lesbian, and a transman can be heterosexual or gay (or bi, in both cases).

Outside of the transgender community, however, many of these terms – and the explanations behind them – are viewed with suspicion. Most of this suspicion centers around the debate regarding the "true" gender identity of transpeople. Is a transwoman really a woman, or a man trying to look and act like a woman? If a male-to-female transsexual has relationships with men, does that make that person heterosexual (because she's really a woman) or gay (because he's really a feminine man)? If we assume that she's female and therefore heterosexual, should she be accepted by the gay community? Challenging questions – and in order to understand the context of these questions, we need to delve into a little bit of history.

————————————————

Nineteen sixty-nine – the Summer of Love. In June of that year, during the early morning hours, police raided a gay bar in Greenwich Village called the Stonewall Inn. Police raids on gay bars were a fairly routine occurrence, but this time was different. Instead of complying with the police, the patrons of the bar fought back, initiating what are now known as the Stonewall Riots, and kicking off the gay and lesbian rights movement. Interestingly, the black sheep of the gay and lesbian community – the cross-dressing street queens – are reported to have been the ones who started the riots. Despite initiating one of the biggest social movements in history, transgender people still live on the fringes of the gay and lesbian community, and continue to fight to be included. In San Francisco, for example, the yearly event that was once known as "Gay Freedom Day" and then the "International Lesbian and Gay Freedom Day Parade" wasn't renamed to include "transgender" until 1995.[87]

While most gay pride celebrations around the world have begun to include the word "transgender" in the title of the event, many transgender people still feel marginalized. In the words of one organizer for the Washington, D.C. Trans Pride event, one of only a few across the U.S., "The transgender community needs its own event, rather than just using us as entertainment. That's all we've been allowed to do."[88] Transpeople were certainly more than entertainment in June of 1969, that's for sure.

Why are transpeople so marginalized in the gay community, despite the fact that they took center stage during the Stonewall Riots? The mobilizers of the gay and lesbian rights movement were the prostitutes, the drug dealers, the gay street teens – figures of the gay and lesbian underworld. For middle-class gay people who want acceptance within mainstream heterosexual culture, men in dresses don't further the goal very effectively (particularly if those men are homeless, prostitutes, and/or drug dealers). However, this likely isn't the only reason transpeople experience an uneasy acceptance (at best) from the gay and lesbian community. Transgender people (particularly transwomen) tend to evoke intense discomfort, for they call into question our deeply entrenched values regarding sex and gender – and what it means to be male or female.

I think it's fair to say that a man in a dress makes

most men feel extremely uncomfortable. For that matter, a man wearing pink, even if it's a tie, probably evokes a similar feeling. Young boys get teased relentlessly if they're wearing something that seems "girly," or if they choose to play with "girl toys." I've seen many a man shudder when his young toddler son is given a doll to play with. And most men wouldn't be caught dead going to a movie theater to see a "chick flick." All of these involve *femiphobia* – the male fear of the feminine. Of course, it's quite easy to spot examples of femiphobia in mainstream heterosexual culture – and ways men protect their sense of masculinity from the feminine. In his film of the same name, Jackson Katz describes the "tough guise" men adopt in order to prove their manhood.[89] Stephen Ducat identifies "the wimp factor" – the fear that Americans are going soft and becoming too feminine as the driving force in right-wing American politics.[90] If a man expresses any hint of femininity, it evokes the fear that his "man card" will be taken away from him.

And yet, when it comes to gay men and masculinity, all bets are off. Or are they? Is a feminine man a "real man"? For that matter, are all gay men by definition feminine? The image of the effeminate gay man has become archetypal in our culture. Limp wrists, high-pitched lispy voices, and a flair for the dramatic are well-known stereotypes associated with gay men. And yet, there is a strong contempt for effeminacy in sectors of the gay male community. "No femmes," for example, is a common phrase seen in the personal ads of gay men. This contempt hasn't gone unnoticed by sexual orientation researchers. Michael Bailey documents the ambivalence gay men have about feminine behavior – despite the fact that many of these men have a history of childhood gender nonconformity.[91] Simon LeVay uses the term "femmephobia" to describe gay men's dislike of effeminate men.[92] "Sissyphobia" is the term that Tim Bergling uses to describe this intense aversion.[93] This aversion is so strong that feminine gay and bisexual males are significantly more likely to attempt suicide than their masculine counterparts.[94] If gay men hope to assimilate, to be accepted as "real men" – and to accept themselves – then purging the feminine from oneself and from the community is essential – both literally and figuratively.

Sadly, another strain of transphobia emerged from the queer community – this one also rooted in femiphobia. To understand the context of this strain, we again need to revisit the 1960s Stonewall era. In tandem with the Stonewall-inspired gay rights movement (along with other historically unprecedented social movements), women's liberation was taking off like wildfire. And yet, lesbian women lived on the fringes of both movements; homophobia in the (heterosexual) women's movement and gynophobia in the male-dominated gay rights movement prevented lesbians from really feeling like a part of either one. A movement of their own, which took the form of lesbian-separatism, thus began to emerge. Practicing lesbian-separatism involved cutting ties with all forms of male privilege as a way of subverting patriarchy. "Feminism is the theory, lesbianism is the practice," was a popular slogan that emerged from this movement. Women who participated in heterosexual relationships – or women who had any ties to men at all, including gay men – were seen as co-conspirators with the enemy. Femininity was seen by lesbian separatists as a political straitjacket, constraining women within the binds of patriarchy. Short hair and flannel shirts were the antidote to dresses, heels, and makeup. Lesbian-separatists created their own communities, publications, and social spaces, all of which had a "no men allowed" policy.

So what happens if a transwoman – who isn't accepted by mainstream culture, and who feels hostility from the gay male community – wants to enter a lesbian-separatist space? If transwomen experienced ambivalence from the gay male community, they were met with out-and-out hostility from lesbian separatists. In 1979, a women's studies professor by the name of Janice Raymond published *The Transsexual Empire: The Making of the She-Male*, which detailed the lesbian-feminist stance on transsexualism with disturbing clarity. Raymond argues that transsexuals, primarily male-to-female transsexuals, are part of an insidious male plot to undermine the women's movement. By wearing makeup and dresses, they are crippling the efforts of feminists to free themselves from the binds of femininity. By undergoing sex-reassignment surgery, MTF transsexuals are symbolically raping women's bodies "by reducing the female form to an artifact, appropriating this body for themselves."[95] In Raymond's eyes, transsexual women are not women – they are referred to as "she-males" or "male-to-constructed females."[96]   In fact, transsexual women are active collaborators with the enemy, and they are, in Raymond's words, "infiltrating the sisterhood to destabilize it."[97] Physicians who perform sex-reassignment surgery aren't let off the hook – Raymond accuses them of being part of the male conspiracy to overthrow the feminist movement, and she compares these surgeons to Nazi death-camp doctors. Female-to-male transsexuals, on the other hand, are given a little more sympathy, for Raymond sees them as victims of the patriarchy, having assimilated themselves into the world of men.

To the transgender community, *The Transsexual Empire* was the most offensive book ever to be published about transsexuals. Reviewers on Amazon.com, for example, have characterized it as a "book of hate," "a transphobic form of radical feminism," "a sophomoric rant," and "a paranoid essentialist classic."[98] Yet if there was such a thing as a "transgender bestseller list," *The*

Transsexual Empire would be on it. It is one of the most widely read books in the transgender community. One website characterizes it as one of two books that sits on the transgender "shelf of shame."[99] And Raymond's ideology has had a very powerful impact on the transgender community.

Much of the transphobia directed at transsexuals stems from the belief that transwomen aren't "real" women. For example, transwomen are often prevented from using women's public restrooms. Transwomen who are homeless may be denied access to shelters geared specifically towards women and children. Transwomen who are trying to escape an abusive relationship may not have access to a battered women's shelter. The list goes on and on. Barred from entering women's spaces in mainstream culture, transwomen might try to seek refuge in lesbian and gay spaces – to no avail, if we use the Michigan Womyn's Music Festival as an example. The MWMF, a lesbian-feminist inspired event, has what is referred to as a "womyn-born-womyn" policy; in other words, those who were born and raised as girls, and who currently identify as women, may attend the festival. According to this policy, transsexual women aren't "real" women, and so they are not welcome. To enforce this policy, "panty checks" were performed for a period of time, and eventually that gave way to a "don't ask, don't tell" policy. In protest of this policy, transgender activists set up Camp Trans, a demonstration that is held outside of the festival grounds.[100] Despite these activist efforts, public statements issued by the MWMF organizers indicate that they still enforce the "WBW" policy.[101]

So transwomen can't enter women's restrooms because they're not "real" women. They can't attend the Michigan Womyn's Music Festival (at least not as an open transsexual) because they aren't "real" women. And yet, the whole argument around performing sex-reassignment surgery has centered on the idea that a transsexual really is a "real" woman – psychologically, emotionally, and spiritually – trapped in a man's physical body. This is the classic transsexual narrative, and the transsexuals who fit this narrative are the ones who are most likely to get approved for surgery. Clearly, some members of mainstream culture aren't buying it. The lesbian-separatists aren't buying it. And some members of the medical community aren't buying it either, the most notable example being Paul McHugh, chief of psychiatry at Johns Hopkins University Hospital, where John Money's famous Gender Identity Clinic is housed.

McHugh, a practicing Catholic and cultural conservative, is the diametrical opposite of lesbian-separatist Janice Raymond. And yet, Raymond and McHugh do agree on this – that transsexual women are not "real women," and that sex-reassignment surgery is a dangerous and inappropriate practice. For McHugh, performing sex-reassignment surgery is like giving liposuction to an anorexic, reinforcing the delusion that the anorexic is fat and her body needs to be corrected. A transsexual doesn't need surgery to create a female body to align with the psychological sense of being female, because he's not really female in the first place:

> Men (and until recently they were all men) with whom I spoke before their surgery would tell me that their bodies and sexual identities were at variance. Those I met after surgery would tell me that the surgery and hormone treatments that had made them 'women' had also made them happy and contented. None of these encounters were persuasive, however. The post-surgical subjects struck me as caricatures of women. They wore high heels, copious makeup, and flamboyant clothing; they spoke about how they found themselves able to give vent to their natural inclinations for peace, domesticity, and gentleness—but their large hands, prominent Adam's apples, and thick facial features were incongruous (and would become more so as they aged). Women psychiatrists whom I sent to talk with them would intuitively see through the disguise and the exaggerated postures. 'Gals know gals,' one said to me, 'and that's a guy.'[102]

So McHugh, like Raymond, doesn't believe that

transsexuals are "real women." And shortly after he became chief of psychiatry at Johns Hopkins Hospital, he shut down Money's famous Gender Identity Clinic and effectively ended the practice of sex-reassignment surgery at that institution. Now, Johns Hopkins has what is called the Sexual Behaviors Consultation Unit, which treats sexual dysfunctions and paraphilias (socially deviant sexual practices, such as exhibitionism, voyeurism, fetishism, and sadomasochism) as well as gender identity concerns. However, their treatment approach for gender identity disorder does not involve any form of surgery.

The Transsexual Empire has certainly left its stamp on the transgender community. And a lot has happened since its publication. For one thing, a trend towards viewing sex-reassignment surgery as a valid and healthy option began to emerge. Despite Raymond's diatribe against sex-reassignment surgery (and McHugh's choice to halt the practice of SRS at Johns Hopkins), today there are a number of clinics in the United States and around the world that offer SRS. We can certainly see the results of these standards in action in the wealth of personal memoirs that have been published in the last several years: *She's Not There* by Jennifer Finney Boylan, *Wrapped in Blue* by Donna Rose, and *Conundrum* by Jan Morris are just a few examples. More and more people are coming out of the closet and living openly as transsexuals. Increasingly, civil rights protections are being granted to transgender people, mainly in the form of workplace protection from discrimination. And some interesting research has been conducted that sheds light on the transsexual experience.

Recall that the single-most powerful strategy the gay and lesbian community has wielded to advocate for their civil rights has been to prove that sexual orientation isn't a choice. Simon LeVay, of course, attempted to do just that through his INAH-3 research, which rested on the assumption that gay men, biologically speaking, are more like heterosexual women than heterosexual men. If gay men are biologically similar to heterosexual women, wouldn't it make sense that male-to-female transsexuals share biological similarities with women as well? That was the question that Dick Swaab and his colleagues set out to investigate.

It is well-established that sexual differentiation of genitals occurs during the first few months of pregnancy – during the early stages of pregnancy, male and female embryos look virtually identical, and differentiate only in the presence of SRY, a portion of the Y chromosome, and testosterone. If sex hormones influence the development of genitals and reproductive organs, scientists theorized, they might just possibly affect brain development, so that our brains become "sexed" just like our physical bodies do. This line of reasoning focused more specifically on the presence of androgens during prenatal development, and much of the research centers around differences in the hypothalamus, the literal and figurative "nerve center" of the sexual brain. The hypothalamus is clearly linked to sexual motivation and sexual behavior, and, although there is controversy surrounding this idea, there do appear to be sex differences in parts of this structure. Swaab and his colleagues became interested in an area of the hypothalamus called the "bed nucleus of the stria terminalis" – a mouthful that can be more easily abbreviated as BSTc. According to their research, males tend to have a BSTc that is twice as large as that as females, and the male BSTc contains double the number of neurons than that of females. This difference is probably established during prenatal development, due to the presence or absence of androgens. Applying this finding to transsexualism, Swaab and his colleagues discovered that male-to-female transsexuals have a female-sized BSTc, again lending credence to the idea that gay men and transwomen share biological commonalities with women.[103]

This finding was the beacon of light for many transgender activists, particularly those active in transgender health care issues. Transgender activists had been fighting for years for things like health insurance coverage for sex-reassignment surgery, and this finding provided a sound scientific rationale for it. If male-to-female transsexuals have a "birth defect" in a sense (a loaded term, to be sure), then they should have the right to have it surgically corrected. And if male-to-female transsexuals are "born that way," then they shouldn't be punished and oppressed for their gender nonconformity.

So the transsexual narrative lives on. "I'm a woman trapped in a man's body, and I've felt that way ever since I can remember. I was probably born that way. I need to live as a woman, in a woman's body, in order to feel whole, complete, and authentic, and I need sex reassignment surgery in order to accomplish that." Transsexual women are, in fact, "real women," despite what Janice Raymond and Paul McHugh have to say. Despite their male physical bodies, they *know* they're female, just like many gay men know at an early age that they're gay, even before they really know the meaning of the word.

Is this really the final word? Read on.

Twenty-five years after the publication of *The Transsexual Empire*, the second of the two books sitting on the transgender "shelf of shame" was published, this one by Michael Bailey – who always seems to find himself at the epicenter of controversy. Bailey's book, titled *The Man Who Would Be Queen*, focuses on gender nonconformity in gay men as well as male-to-female transsexuals. The first two parts of his book provides a user-friendly overview of his own research, mostly focusing on gender nonconformity and homosexuality in men. His discussion of the research is peppered with personal stories and vignettes, in an attempt to bring the science to life. In the last third of the book, Bailey departs from his own research and focuses more specifically on male-to-female transsexualism, taking the opportunity to challenge the "standard transsexual narrative." It was this section of the book that sparked a firestorm of controversy. In fact, that's probably an understatement – reactions to his theories of male-to-female transsexualism have moved beyond the confines of academic debate and into the realm of an all-out Jerry Springer-style brawl. And I'm not exaggerating.

Bailey focuses on the work of Ray Blanchard, who heads up the Clinical Sexology Program of the Clarke Institute of Psychiatry in Toronto. The Clarke follows what is known as the Standards of Care for gender identity disorders, developed in 1979 by the Harry Benjamin International Gender Dysphoria Association (now known as the World Professional Association for Transgender Health). The Standards of Care are a set of requirements that individuals must meet in order to qualify for hormone replacement therapy and sex-reassignment surgery. These requirements include receiving the diagnosis from a psychiatrist or psychologist of Gender Identity Disorder (which involves experiencing cross-gender feelings or engaging in cross-gender behaviors); undergoing a significant period of psychotherapy; and completing the "Real-Life Experience," where the individual lives full-time as a member of their opposite assigned sex. The Clarke is well-known among transgender activists for using a stricter form of the Standards of Care, for utilizing a medical/pathological model of gender identity disorder, and, most notably, for introducing the concept of the autogynephilic transsexual.[104]

Based on his research conducted at the Clarke, Blanchard distinguishes between two types of transsexuals. Homosexual transsexuals are extremely feminine gay men. Instead of hiding their femininity, or living comfortably as a feminine man, most of them decide to transition and live full-time as women. Members of the transgender community would likely call these people heterosexual transwomen, because they fit the "women trapped in men's bodies" narrative. They tend to have histories of childhood gender nonconformity. In adolescence and adulthood, homosexual transsexuals tend to be attracted to straight men. They also tend to have histories of cross-dressing, although they rarely reported having a sexual response to it. Most people aren't surprised when homosexual transsexuals "come out," because their femininity is obvious.[105]

Autogynephilic transsexuals, on the other hand, are men who have an erotic response to the idea of themselves as women. It is related to the DSM-IV diagnosis of transvestic fetishism, a paraphilia which involves a sexual and erotic interest in cross-dressing. Autogynephilia takes this a step further; not only are autogynephiles sexually attracted to cross-dressing, they are aroused by the idea of having a vulva, or of being penetrated by a penis. Autogynephiles tend to be masculine boys during childhood, and they continue to be masculine in their adolescence and adulthood. Most get married, have children, and work in masculine occupations (both Bailey and Blanchard observe an overrepresentation of autogynephiles who work in scientific or technological fields). They are also less likely, after transitioning to life as a woman, to "pass" well; they just don't look like women. They are not women trapped in men's bodies.[106] Instead, in Bailey's words, they "are men who have created their image of attractive women in their own bodies, an image that coexists with their original, male selves. The female self is a man-made creation."[107]

If you think this sounds reminiscent of Janice Raymond's "male-to-constructed females" concept, the memory of *The Transsexual Empire* likely echoed in the minds of many a transsexual upon reading *The Man*

Who Would Be Queen. Clearly, if autogynephilia became
an accepted explanation of transsexualism, then the
"I'm a woman trapped in a man's body" narrative
would no longer hold water. For autogynephiles, sex-
reassignment surgery wouldn't achieve a congruent
gender identity – instead, it would fulfill their sexual
and erotic motivations. Presenting oneself as a woman
trapped in a man's body is likely to lead to approval for
sex reassignment surgery. Presenting oneself as a man
who is sexually aroused by the idea of being a woman
probably would not. And this drew the ire of the
transgender community. What also invoked the wrath of
transgender activists is that there seemed to be no room
for disagreement. "Some autogynephilic individuals
are prone to denying autogynephilia," Bailey states
on his website.[108] According to Blanchard's research,
"transsexuals who deny being either homosexual or
autogynephilic are probably autogynephilic."[109] So the
stories of transsexuals are not to be trusted.

Shortly after Bailey's book was published, a
tidal wave of opposition began to crest. A group of
transsexual activists launched an all-out smear campaign
against Bailey. This went significantly above and beyond
the typical debate a controversial theory might generate
– even beyond some of the personal attacks researchers
like Simon LeVay experienced. Charges of scientific
misconduct, including lack of informed consent, failure

to obtain institutional approval for the research, and having sex with a transsexual research subject, were levied against Bailey. He was then subjected to a top-level investigation at Northwestern University (and was eventually cleared). Protests were staged in response to the book's nomination for a Lambda Literary Foundation award. Other scientific researchers were discouraged from having any association with Bailey, particularly if they were applying for any type of research funding. At its worst, his children, his ex-wife, and other people in Bailey's life were harassed and intimidated via the Internet.[110]

Alice Dreger's involvement in the Bailey controversy began in 2006. A researcher at the Feinberg School of Medicine at Northwestern University and former co-director of ISNA (Intersex Society of North America), Dreger had been called on by transgender activists to get involved on their behalf in the controversy – largely because of her intersex activism. Having never read the book before, and having never met Bailey, Dreger was prepared to view Bailey as a "homophobic, transphobic, sloppy scientist."[111] Upon meeting Bailey and finding him to be "intelligent, open-minded, scientifically careful, and non-homophobic,"[112] Dreger became increasingly curious about the controversy, particularly since Bailey presented quite differently than the caricature that was painted of him. She then involved herself in a year-long investigation of the Bailey controversy; fifty-six pages detailing the results of this investigation were published in the *Archives of Sexual Behavior*. In general, Dreger concluded that the rules of academic debate had been broken, that the accusations hurled at Bailey were groundless, and that debate surrounding a controversial theory quickly deteriorated into an ugly, malicious personal vendetta against Bailey.[113] Ironically, as a result of her involvement in the Bailey controversy, Dreger herself has become the target of transsexual activists who are attempting to ruin and discredit her.

To be sure, Dreger noted that "Bailey stuck his hand into a buzzing hornet's nest, and he should have expected to be stung." [114] And Dreger stuck her hand into the hornet's nest herself. Why was this such a hornet's nest? Certainly transgender people have been one of the most marginalized and oppressed groups of people. They are denied adequate health care. They are subjected to workplace harassment and employment discrimination. Many transsexuals end up doing sex work, including exotic dancing, pornography, and prostitution. They are subjected to the most violent hate crimes in the LGBT community. According to one source, one out of every 1,000 murders in the U.S. involves a transsexual.[115] Their motives have been questioned repeatedly. They have been diagnosed, pathologized, put into numerous typologies and categories. Any theory that offers a less-than-attractive perspective on transsexualism would of course be viewed with suspicion. Unfortunately, because this is such a politically charged topic, and because there is such pressure for researchers and activists to stay "on message" regarding the transsexual narrative, the truth may never be known. In light of that, it's hard to know whether the "woman in a man's body" story is in fact the truth, or if it's the cover story designed to appeal to the masses.

Will we ever know the truth? Is it really true that transsexuals are women trapped in men's bodies, or men trapped in women's bodies? Or is there a completely different phenomenon going on?

7

TOPPLING THE TOWER OF BABEL

Transsexuals are trapped in the body of the wrong sex.

Transsexuals are either gay and feminine, or they are fulfilling their sexual urges through their cross-gender behavior.

Transsexuals are part of the conspiracy to overthrow the feminist movement.

Transsexual women are real women.

Transsexual "women" are anything but women – they're just a caricature of what we expect women to be.

As radically different as these theories are, they all rest on the same assumption – the idea that only two categories exist: male and female. Of course, this is a fair assumption to make. When a baby is born, the first question everyone asks is, "What is it?" A silly question, since it's obviously a baby – but we all know what we're *really* asking: we want to know whether it's a girl or a boy. In fact, we get so anxious about not knowing the sex of our baby that we've developed all sorts of technologies to help us identify the sex as soon as possible – in some cases, as early as ten weeks into a pregnancy. And when we ask the question, "What is it?" we're expecting one of two answers. Never would we expect the response to be, "Oh, it doesn't really matter," or "We don't know," or "It's something in-between." But what if there is something in-between? What if our male-female typology is inaccurate?

In the wake of the transsexual narrative, the Bailey/Blanchard typology, and Janice Raymond's lesbian-feminist manifesto, a progressive shift has taken place among many transgender activists. Instead of rehashing the "real man/real woman" argument, activists like Kate Bornstein, Patrick Califia, Leslie Feinberg, and Joan Nestle question the binary male-female system, and argue instead that gender is a malleable and socially constructed category. Gender identity is variegated, rather than monochromatic, and seeing gender as a one-or-the-other phenomenon limits our freedom to express our true identities.

They don't just argue the point – they live it. In

Gender Outlaw, Kate Bornstein says, "I know I'm not a man – about that much I'm very clear, and I've come to the conclusion that I'm probably not a woman either, at least not according to a lot of people's rules on this sort of thing. The trouble is, we're living in a world that insists that we be one or the other – a world that doesn't bother to tell us exactly what one or the other is."[116] Patrick Califia, who is best known for his S/M activism within the lesbian community, said the following regarding his own gender transition: "I can't tell you that I 'feel like a man trapped in a woman's body' because that isn't true. What I feel like is a transgendered person. And what I call myself now is a bisexual transgendered person, who will probably be living socially as a man sometime in the next year or two. I think I'll always be somewhat gender ambiguous." Califia goes on to say, "I feel like I can put on a credible performance as both a woman and as a man, and at various points in my life have done both of those things. But neither one is really a very good fit for me."[117] Leslie Feinberg says, "I am a human being who would rather not be addressed as Ms. or Mr., ma'am or sir. I prefer to use gender-neutral pronouns like *sie* (pronounced like 'see') or *hir* (pronounced like 'here') to describe myself. I am a person who faces insurmountable difficulty when instructed to check off an 'F' or an 'M' box on identification papers."[118] These are people who live beyond our traditional gender categories, in the area between pink and blue.

Is this even possible? What happens when a person deliberately chooses *not* to choose "M" or "F"? Not knowing a person's sex makes us extremely uncomfortable. For those of us who watched *Saturday Night Live* during the early 1990s undoubtedly remember Julia Sweeney's gender-ambiguous character "Pat." In these skits, everyone tries to figure out what "Pat" is without being rude or offensive – to no avail. Pat's vague responses to these attempts are an endless source of frustration, and in the end we never find out whether Pat is male or female. The comedy in this sketch lies in our discomfort – we laugh because deep down, we find Pat's gender ambiguity to be deeply unsettling. And this is reality for people who live outside the margins of traditional gender categories.

While laughter was our collective response to Pat, fear and violence are the more likely reaction to gender ambiguity. It's no anomaly that Joan of Arc was burned at the stake for wearing masculine clothing. Drag queens, feminine gay men, butch women, and people who are not clearly identifiable as male or female are frequently the targets of violent hate crimes. Brandon Teena, whose life and violent death were the subject of the Academy-award winning film *Boys Don't Cry*, was assaulted, raped, and subsequently murdered for being trans.[119] Even an association with a transgender person is risky: Barry Winchell, an infantry soldier in the U.S. Army, was beaten to death because of his relationship with transwoman Calpernia Addams – a crime that became known as the "don't ask, don't tell" murder.[120] Violating gender categories has serious, potentially fatal, consequences.

And, as with homosexuality, the Bible weighs in on the issue of gender-bending as well. The book of Deuteronomy, part of which outlines the law of God, has two references forbidding gender nonconformity. Deuteronomy 22:5 states, "The woman shall not wear that which pertaineth unto a man, neither shall a man put on a woman's garment: for all that do so are abomination unto the Lord thy God." And Deuteronomy 23:1 says, "He that is wounded in the stones, or hath his privy member cut off, shall not enter into the congregation of the Lord." Violating the law of God results in being sent to Hell.

Yet there are numerous historical and cross-cultural examples of traversing male-female gender lines – and at one time, in many cultures, a palette of gender expressions was common and sometimes even celebrated. Probably the best example of this lies in the Two-Spirit traditions of many Native American tribes. These were people who embodied the concept of gender fluidity – the idea that one's gender expression can change over time, and that gender expression need not align with anatomy and genitalia. Two-Spirit people, viewed as possessing spiritual gifts and healing powers, often served as shamans and medicine men within their tribes. Within these traditions, multiple and varied gender expressions were revered and respected, rather than condemned. At least this was the case until the Europeans came to the Americas and attempted to colonize Native people. The European colonizers, who used the derogatory term *berdache* to refer to Two-Spirits, did everything in their power to fit Native people within a two-category sex/gender system. These attempts ranged from removing children from their tribes and sending them to boarding schools, incarcerating Two-Spirits and forcing them to present themselves in a gender-conforming way, and, at its worst, slaughtering people who violated the western European two-category sex/gender system.

Other gender-nonconforming traditions continue to exist in various cultures around the world. In parts of South Asia, including India, Pakistan, and Bangladesh, there exists a "third gender," referred to as a *hijra*. A hijra, usually a biological male or intersex person, is seen as neither man nor woman. They dress as female and engage in feminine behaviors, although they make no attempts to pass as women. Some undergo emasculation, involving the removal of the penis, testes, and scrotum, through a ritual ceremony initiating them into the "hijra family." Like many transpeople in the United States, hijras live on the margins of society. They face multiple forms of discrimination, including in employment, housing, and health care, and they are frequently the targets of violent hate crimes. In Thailand, a *kathoey*, colloquially known as "ladyboy," is a male who exhibits varying degrees of femininity. They might be feminine gay males, or they may cross-dress and undergo the gender reassignment process. They tend to work in feminine occupations, and are heavily represented in the sex work industry. While kathoeys generally enjoy greater acceptance in Thailand than their transwomen counterparts do in the U.S., they are not legally recognized in Thailand.

In some cultures, engaging in gender-nonconforming behaviors results in social privilege rather than ostracism and oppression. For example, in Albania and Montenegro, a s*worn* or *pledged virgin* is a biological female who takes on the male social role, but pledges lifelong sexual abstinence and remains unmarried. By taking on the masculine role, sworn virgins gain social privileges denied to women who remain in their feminine role, such as smoking, using guns, and attending male-only events. This practice is intended to preserve the patriarchal tradition in these cultures in the event that no males are born to a family, or if war or other political skirmishes result in a shortage of males.

If gender nonconformity is so common around the world and throughout history, why have there been such forceful attempts to fit people into "male" and "female" boxes? According to Leslie Feinberg, creating gendered categories and forcing people to fit into one or the other was one of a wide range of attempts throughout history to control and colonize the "savages," "heathens," and the "uncultured."[121] Feinberg's well-researched book *Transgender Warriors* provides an in-depth history of transsexualism and gender-bending, tracing the roots of oppression to colonization, the overthrow of communalism, and the rise of class divisions. Whatever the historical origins, the seeds of transphobia that were planted centuries ago have remained deeply rooted. Our reliance on male-female categories has even extended to inanimate objects. Ask any child to categorize toys, clothing, or colors into "masculine" or "feminine," and they will do so without blinking an eye. When it comes to categorizing people into "male" and "female," the limitations of these categories (and the consequences of trying to squeeze people into them) become abundantly clear with respect to intersexuality.

Intersexuality is the biological gray area between male and female. A person who is intersex doesn't clearly fit, biologically speaking, into the category of "male" or "female." Some people might be more familiar with the term *hermaphrodite* (now considered to be a derogatory term), although it is physically impossible to be both fully male and fully female. An intersex person may look female on the outside, but have an XY (male) chromosomal pattern. Or an intersex person might have an atypical chromosomal pattern which creates masculinizing or feminizing effects. Some intersex conditions are identified at birth, while others might not be diagnosed until adolescence or adulthood. Despite the fact that intersex conditions are common (the Intersex Society of North America cites one in 100 births in which a variation from standard male or female exists),[122] many people have never heard of intersex, and quite a few intersex people have had their condition concealed from them (for reasons we'll discuss in a minute).

Several intersex conditions are due to a chromosomal anomaly. Klinefelter syndrome, for example, occurs when an XXY chromosomal pattern results in a small penis and testes, breast development, and an absence of facial hair. Turner's syndrome is a condition in which only one sex chromosome is present (an X); this causes the external genitalia to look female, although other female characteristics are absent or underdeveloped. More commonly, intersex conditions involve the sex hormones, particularly the androgens. For example, androgen insensitivity syndrome (AIS) occurs in XY males whose bodies don't respond normally to the presence of sex hormones. As a result, these individuals look and are usually labeled female at birth; their condition usually isn't detected until the absence of menstruation raises questions in adolescence. Another condition, congenital adrenal hyperplasia, occurs in XX females who lack an enzyme necessary to build an adrenal hormone called cortisol, which ultimately results in a buildup of testosterone and progesterone. These hormones create masculinizing effects, including a large clitoris, facial hair, deepening of the voice, and higher-than-average muscle mass. A less common (albeit fascinating) condition, 5-alpha reductase deficiency involves, in XY males, the absence of an enzyme that converts testosterone to dihydrotestosterone (DHT). At birth, these babies are typically labeled as girls; however, once they hit adolescence, testosterone production causes their bodies to masculinize (hence the moniker "penis-at-12"). These are literally children who begin their lives as females and then, at puberty, see their bodies masculinizing before their very eyes.

My students are fascinated by intersex conditions. Most of them had never heard of such a thing, and while many can easily understand the idea of transsexualism, for some reason they have a much harder time digesting the fact that biological factors can result in gender ambiguity. They are even more fascinated – and disturbed – by the fact that, if the ISNA odds are correct, they probably know someone who is intersex. In class, when we're having a discussion about this, my students routinely have trouble leaving this topic and moving on to a different one. It must be like watching a car wreck – they're disturbed by it, but they can't tear their gaze away from it. When we talk about transsexualism, my students' acceptance of the two-gender system usually goes unchallenged, because they don't typically see transsexuals as a "third gender" – they're one gender trapped in the body of the other gender. When we talk about intersex, however, the accuracy of these two categories comes into question. And to have our gendered worldview completely overthrown is deeply unsettling.

The medical community has been rigidly accepting of the two-category classification system – particularly at clinics that specialize in "treating" intersex conditions. For decades, the medical profession has relied on what is referred to as the "Hopkins model," named for the medical team at Johns Hopkins that developed the "optimum gender of rearing" system for treating children with intersex conditions. This model, which rested upon the theories of psychologist John Money, involved assigning a gender to an intersex child as early as possible and, if necessary, performing cosmetic genital surgery and/or administering hormones in order to align the child's physical body with the assigned gender identity. The choice of gender identity didn't matter, according to this

model, because any child could be "made" into a girl or a
boy by performing genital surgery and then subsequently
raising the child as their assigned sex. Growing up healthy
and well-adjusted doesn't require choosing the "correct"
gender identity – it merely requires that children's bodies
needed to be consistent with their gender label, and
that they be socialized appropriately. Many doctors who
treat intersex children have relied upon a concealment-
centered model, in which the child's intersex history (and
treatments) are withheld from the child – the rationale
being that knowing about their intersex condition and
treatments would result in gender identity confusion.

So, in this view, nurture trumps nature. Or does
it? Is it possible to choose wrong? Does a concealment-
centered model protect the child from – or unintentionally
invoke – psychological harm? The experiences of David
Reimer and Cheryl Chase provide disquieting clarity to
these questions.

––––––––––

Bruce and Brian Reimer were twin boys who
were born in 1965. At eight months old, Bruce was
the unfortunate victim of a botched circumcision that
resulted in the loss of his entire penis. His doctors
predicted that Bruce would be psychologically damaged
by the absence of his penis, and a phalloplasty (penile

reconstruction) was subsequently recommended. Of course, surgical techniques have been improved so that artificially constructed penises look realistic – but in 1965, phalloplasty techniques were crude and didn't yield promising results. Bruce's parents, who were obviously upset about Bruce's prognosis, were hesitant to go through with such a surgery. Then, one night, they saw a TV show featuring John Money, who talked about his approach to gender reassignment. The show featured transsexuals and intersex children, and it showcased how Money relied on the tools of hormones and surgery to make children into whatever sex seemed best. That TV show probably felt like a message from God, for it provided an alternative to phalloplasty (or living with a mutilated penis). The Reimers wrote a letter to Money, and that began their long relationship with Money and the Johns Hopkins Gender Identity Clinic.[123]

Money was a pioneer in the area of intersexuality and gender identity. He built his career at Johns Hopkins on the idea that newborns are a blank slate when it comes to gender. By the time the Reimers came to see Money, he had the firmly established reputation as *the* authority on intersex and gender identity conditions. Nobody dared question Money's theories, despite decades of research on the role of chromosomes and hormones in determining sexual behavior and gender identity. And so it was no surprise that Bruce's parents followed Money's advice – which was to have him surgically castrated and raise him as a girl – to the letter. Bruce underwent the surgery, and thus "Brenda" was born.

    Man and Woman, Boy and Girl, published in 1973, was Money's first written account of Bruce's case. Using the pseudonyms "John" and "Joan," Money's portrayal of the case suggested that it was a complete success.[124] Two years later, in the *Archives of Sexual Behavior*, Money asserted, "No one [outside the family] knows [that she was born a boy]. Nor would they ever conjecture. Her behavior is so normally that of an active little girl, and so clearly different by contrast from the boyish ways of her twin brother, that it offers nothing to stimulate one's conjectures."[125] That same year, Money published *Sexual Signatures: On Being a Man or Woman*, a book intended to reach a wider general readership. Again, Money described Joan's case as "dramatic proof that the gender-identity option is open at birth for normal infants."[126] That statement, and his portrayal of the case as a whole, legitimized the practice of infant sex reassignment and firmly entrenched the "Hopkins model" within the medical community. Moreover, Money's accounts appealed strongly to liberal feminists, who advocated that sex differences (and oppression based on those differences) were due entirely to socialization within a patriarchal system. Psychology, sociology, and women's studies texts were revised in order to incorporate the success of the John/Joan case.

This case came at just the right time for Money. Despite his ironclad reputation, Money's work was not immune to criticism. As early as 1965, a young graduate student by the name of Milton Diamond found evidence linking prenatal hormonal exposure to later sexual functioning. Subsequently, he published a critique of Money's theories in *The Quarterly Review of Biology*, where he argued that gender identity is neurologically hard-wired from conception. At the end of his paper, Diamond offered Money a challenge: "To support [such a] theory, we have been presented with no instance of a normal individual appearing as an unequivocal male and being reared successfully as a female."[127] A year and a half later, the Reimers' letter documenting Bruce's tragic surgical accident was delivered to Money's mailbox, providing him with just the opportunity to prove Diamond wrong.

Was Diamond wrong? For several years, there was no doubt in anyone's mind (except maybe Diamond's) that the case was nothing but an unequivocal success. In 1976, due to problems in school, Brenda was referred to the Child Guidance Clinic, where she met with several psychiatrists, including Dr. Keith Sigmundson. Sigmundson couldn't ignore the obvious signs of masculinity Brenda was exhibiting – she looked like a boy, talked like a boy, acted like a boy. There was nothing feminine about her at all. Unsettled by the case,

Sigmundson contacted Money and informed him of Brenda's school problems and emotional difficulties – to no avail. In fact, Money responded by urging Sigmundson to "help her break down" her fear of hospitals so that the last stage of vaginal surgery (which hadn't been performed in infancy) could be completed. Despite his concern regarding the case, Sigmundson didn't dare cross Money. "I was shit-scared of John Money," he admits. "He was the big guy. The guru. I didn't know what it would do to my career."[128]

Other signs that the case was anything but an unqualified success were beginning to emerge. In 1980, the BBC produced a documentary on the John/Joan case, initially expecting to feature Money with Diamond as representing the "fringe" opinion. To the producers' surprise, when they located "Joan," it was abundantly clear that Joan was anything but well-adjusted. She exhibited obvious signs of masculinity, she was having difficulty in school, and she was ridiculed by her classmates. The BBC aired the documentary without input from Money, and it was the first time that the public became aware that Money's account was not necessarily the truth.[129]

Fourteen years later, Diamond and Sigmundson teamed up to interview "John/Joan" (who, at the time of the interview, had been living as a male), his mother, and his wife. Based on these interviews, Diamond and Sigmundson wrote a paper documenting the true events of the case, arguing that gender identity and sexual orientation are inborn, and not malleable via the sex reassignment process. It was an uphill battle to get the paper published (because of Money's reputation, no one wanted to touch a critique with a ten-foot pole), although it was eventually accepted by the *Archives of Adolescent and Pediatric Medicine*.[130] The paper's publication sparked massive controversy, along the lines of screaming matches rather than academic debates. Not only were Diamond and Sigmundson challenging the existing worldview regarding sexual and gender identity development, they were exposing Money's fraudulent portrayal of the John/Joan case.

When "John/Joan" himself decided to come forward and tell his story, even more harrowing details of the case were revealed. In *As Nature Made Him: The Boy Who Was Raised as a Girl*, John Colapinto documents in unwavering detail the dismal failure of the experiment, and the toll it took on the child. Not only was there no shred of femininity in "Joan," she began to dread the visits to Money's clinic. She and her twin brother always knew on some level that their parents and the doctors were withholding something from them. Joan began resisting going to the appointments, and she could not be convinced to have the remainder of the vaginal surgery (which had nothing to do with a fear of hospitals, but everything to do with the fact that she knew, deep down, that she was not a girl). At age 14, Joan made the decision to live as a male, and he changed his name to David. A year later, his parents made a full disclosure of what had happened to him. His adolescence and early adulthood were peppered with difficulties with dating, and he made two suicide attempts in quick succession. At age 23, he met and later married a single mom with three children.[131] At the time of publication of *As Nature Made Him*, David seemed to be a well-adjusted heterosexual man – but in 2004, at the age of 38, David took his own life.[132]

In 1956, nine years before Reimer was born, a young Catholic housewife was lying in a hospital bed in New Jersey, sedated by the doctors as they prepared to deliver the crushing news about her newborn baby. Three days after birth, this baby with ambiguous genitals still remained genderless. The baby was eventually named Brian Sullivan and lived as a boy for the first 18 months of his life, at which point he was diagnosed as a "true hermaphrodite." As *The New York Times* reports, "Brian was renamed Bonnie, her 'nubbin' (which was either a small penis or a large clitoris) was entirely removed and doctors counseled the family to throw away all pictures of Brian, move to a new town and get on with their lives."[133] The promise of the concealment-centered model was this: "The doctors promised my parents if they did that …that I'd grow up normal, happy, heterosexual and give them grandchildren."[134] Nothing could be further from the truth.

Bonnie's childhood and adolescence was strikingly similar to that of David Reimer. She was depressed throughout this period of her life, and she felt ostracized from her peers, although she could never put her finger on why she felt that way. Other than being told at age 10 that she'd had surgery to remove a large clitoris (which, to a relatively young child, probably sounded like a malignant tumor), Bonnie was told nothing about her condition. And yet, she sensed on some level that there was more to the story. That instinct was confirmed when, at 22 years, Bonnie gained access to her medical records and was pummeled with the truth.

In one of my classes, I ask my students, with a mischievous smile on my face, to raise their hands if they are 100% sure that they are male or female. (Usually everyone raises his or her hand, wondering where I'm going with this). Then I pick a student randomly and ask her to tell me how she knows this. She might laugh uncomfortably and say, "I have breasts and a vagina." Or she might say, "I can give birth," or "I have a menstrual period." Or a male student might note that he has a penis, or male secondary sex characteristics. Invariably a student will say that she has an XX chromosomal pattern, or that he has an XY chromosomal pattern. (I usually take this opportunity to ask how many of the students have ever had a chromosomal test done, just to be sure.) At the end, I ask students this question: "How many of you know that you're male or female because – you just *know*?" And once again, usually everyone raises his or her hand. Most of us don't need elaborate chromosomal or hormonal tests. Most of us don't need to periodically check ourselves out in the mirror to remind us whether we're male or female. We just *know*. And both Bonnie Sullivan and David Reimer *knew* on some level that the gender story they were being told wasn't the truth.

Many people who experience severe trauma flee into addictive behaviors, and Bonnie Sullivan was no exception. She spent the next 13 years of her life living the life of a workaholic, subconsciously digesting the truth of her childhood and adolescence. In the early 1990s, after suffering from a nervous breakdown,[135] Bonnie decided that it was time to lift the heavy emotional weight she was carrying, and she moved to San Francisco – a relatively safe haven for a gender variant. Her recovery began with information-gathering, little of which was readily available at the time. According to *The New York Times*, "[Bonnie] started calling and writing to doctors, academics, and gender activists – anybody who might have something concrete to say about the predicament of being born part male, part female, or who might be able to tell her why it had been necessary to have her clitoris removed and if she'd be able to get any sexual function back."[136]   Along the way, she met many, many people who shared her dirty little secret – the fact that they had surgery performed on them as infants without their consent, and that the nature of their intersex condition was concealed from them. In 1993, Bonnie issued a call to people with intersex conditions to contact her in a letter to *The Sciences*, a magazine that had previously published the work of Anne Fausto-Sterling, a professor of biology and gender studies at Brown University who had substantive knowledge of intersex. This letter marked the turning point in Bonnie's recovery – she signed it "Cheryl Chase, the Intersex Society of North America."[137] And in that action, a wounded individual was reborn, and a groundbreaking organization sprung to life.

The Intersex Society of North America (ISNA) eventually emerged as an advocacy group on behalf of people with intersex conditions, and as a resource for health care providers and for parents to provide comprehensive and accurate information about intersex. ISNA is probably best known for their recommendations regarding the medical treatment of intersex children. These recommendations, crafted with the help of Milton Diamond and Keith Sigmundson, include the following: being truthful with parents and children about the intersex condition and treatment options; providing access to trained mental health professionals and to other forms of intersex support; and – most importantly – giving intersex newborns a gender assignment but delaying genital surgery until the child is mature enough to make the decision for him or herself. Medical and surgical procedures should only be performed to sustain life – not to allay a parent's anxieties or to "cement" a gender identity.[138]

While most of these recommendations seem benign – note that, for example, ISNA does not recommend raising a child as "genderless" or as a "third gender" – the idea of delaying genital surgery is a radical idea to the mainstream medical community. After 13 years of tireless activism and education, the prestigious medical journal *Pediatrics* published a paper in March 2006 that effectively signaled the fall of the "Hopkins model." This paper, titled "Consensus Statement on the Management of Intersex Disorders" and signed by fifty international experts (including Chase), fully endorses the ISNA position on medical treatment of intersex conditions, citing findings from well-designed scientific studies.[139]

Despite the publication of this groundbreaking article, "corrective" genital surgery is still routinely performed in the surgical back rooms. Ignorance regarding intersex conditions is still the norm (although awareness has increased significantly since the early 1990s). And yet, two years after the *Pediatrics* article was published, ISNA closed its doors. ISNA's home page cites a number of reasons for the demise of the organization, including the following: "[W}e finally have consensus on improvements to care for which we have advocated for so long, but we lack a consistent way to implement, monitor, and evaluate them. At present, the new standard of care exists as little more than ideals on paper."[140]

So we have standards, but no way of ensuring that medical professionals actually follow them. Given that the majority of physicians and surgeons still embrace the concealment-centered "Hopkins model" (including John Money himself), this is a serious concern. And yet, why would this be a reason to shut down an organization that has made such a positive impact? The ISNA website addresses this, albeit in a very nebulous way:

> Although [ISNA] has been very successful in recent years in creating collaborative relationships, there is concern among many healthcare professionals, parents, and mainstream healthcare system funders that ISNA's views are biased or that an association with ISNA will be frowned upon by colleagues and peers. And there is widespread misinformation about ISNA's positions.[141]

The site never makes clear what those "biased" views or "widespread misinformation" refers to. However, the narrative on ISNA's website goes on to describe a new organization established in 2008 called Accord Alliance, whose mission is "to promote comprehensive and integrated approaches to care that enhance the health and well-being of people and families affected by DSD by fostering collaboration among all stakeholders."[142] In other words, it brings together health care providers and other constituencies in order to further the goal that ISNA couldn't – to implement, monitor, and evaluate appropriate health care practices for people with intersex conditions. Except on the Accord Alliance website, these conditions aren't called "intersex" anymore – we're now seeing the mysterious term "DSD" (you probably noted those initials in the mission statement). The Consensus Statement published in *Pediatrics*, while breaking ground by endorsing and scientifically validating the ISNA standard of care, evoked controversy by proposing the use of the term "disorders of sex development" or "disorders of sex differentiation." The authors suggest that "terms such as intersex, pseudohermaphroditism, hermaphroditism, sex reversal, and gender-based diagnostic labels are particularly controversial" and may be perceived as confusing and pejorative.[143]

This terminology change appears to have support from many of the intersex community's major players. Cheryl Chase, for example, argues that the term "intersex," while useful from a political standpoint, is ambiguous and confusing. It's a term used differently by different medical practitioners, and it doesn't even mean the same thing to everyone in the intersex and queer communities. Moreover, Chase argues that the apolitical term "DSD" facilitates a conversation with medical practitioners more easily than the very politically-charged term "intersex" does.[144] Alice Dreger (whom you may remember from the previous chapter), an internationally-known researcher, intersex activist, and long-time co-director of ISNA, gives a little more perspective on this:

> When Cheryl Chase founded the Intersex Society of North America (ISNA) in 1993, she used that medical term, and in doing so, she and other early intersex activists gave the term a political valence it hadn't had before. Now "intersex" started to mean something other than—or something more than—a biological state, a medical condition. It began to carry with it a political identity. . . . "Intersex" had a way of feeling totalizing, because it had come to represent an identity. . . . The people who were uncomfortable with intersex wanted to make it go away in children – they didn't want their defenseless babies being drafted into a political identity movement.[145]

Dreger's statements may well shed some light on the "biases" and "widespread misinformation" that caused ISNA to shutter its operations. ISNA began as a grassroots organization dedicated to empowering intersex people. And yet, according to the Organisation Internationale des Intersexues (OII), at the end ISNA "had a membership of 47 people with only 8 intersex individuals amongst them. ISNA's medical advisory board of 26 had no intersex inclusion although it included one psychiatrist, some psychologists, two ethicists, a philosophy of religion professor, a social worker or two and quite a few pediatric endocrinologists. *It seems that everyone is an expert on intersex except intersex people ourselves"* (emphasis added).[146] What began as an activist group became a professional organization, and some intersex activists feel that their group's membership and purpose was hijacked by the mainstream medical community.

It is the shift in purpose that has stirred the pot more than anything else. When Bonnie Sullivan signed a different name and associated herself with the Intersex Society of North America, she claimed a new political identity – and gave birth to a political movement. She wanted to be told the truth about her identity. She wanted to be accepted, rather than mainstreamed. And while the Consensus Statement marked a victory in the 13-year battle that ISNA had been fighting, this publication (and the proposal of the DSD terminology) signaled the end of a political era. Now we're talking about "treating" people with disorders of sex development, instead of accepting intersex people as they are – just like "treating" homosexuality is a far different goal from accepting gay people as they are. "Treatment" is a medical goal; "acceptance" is a political goal. And as we'll see in the next chapter, gay rights activists fought very, very hard to change the view that homosexuality is a pathology that needs changing.

PART III

THE ACTIVISM STORY

8

THE FIRST "GAY ACTIVIST" RESEARCHER

Nineteen fifty-seven. Dwight D. Eisenhower had just entered his second term as President of the United States. Families ate TV dinners while watching *The Adventures of Ozzie and Harriet*, *Leave It to Beaver*, and *American Bandstand*. Schoolchildren were learning to read with the help of *Dick and Jane*. Elvis Presley appeared on *The Ed Sullivan Show* for the third and final time. On the surface, the 1950s was a happy, more innocent, family values-oriented time period in American history. At least from the waist up.

Below the waist, so to speak, the 1950s was a dark period in American history – the age of McCarthyism, if you will. Beneath the squeaky-clean values and imagery portrayed in American culture, a growing fear and paranoia regarding the perceived threat of Communism had reached its height during this era – and the U.S. needed to secure its borders against any type of communist influence. "Communist influence" included any liberal, leftist, or progressive associations, beliefs, or activities – including homosexuality. As chair of the House Committee on Un-American Activities, Rep. Joseph McCarthy (R-WI) was tasked with exposing homosexuals[147] in the government and in the armed forces. Police raids of gay bars, clubs, and parties became routine. Undercover police officers would pose as gay men, and people who were suspected of homosexuality were forced to betray their gay friends and loved ones in order to protect themselves. The names of identified homosexuals were published in newspapers, often resulting in unemployment, loss of housing, divorce, estrangement from family members, and fears for one's personal safety. The "Pink Scare" made for an extremely hostile atmosphere for gays and lesbians. And yet, 1957 marked a turning point regarding the cultural perception of homosexuality.

That turning point came in the very unlikely form of Evelyn Hooker, a woman who came from very humble beginnings. Hooker, the sixth of nine children, spent her early childhood in North Platte, Nebraska, where she was educated in one-room schoolhouses.

Her family was poor, and as a female growing up in the 1910s and 1920s, higher education wouldn't ordinarily have been on the radar screen for a girl like Evelyn – unless there was significant encouragement and support from other women in her life. And that support was there – first from Evelyn's mother, who herself only had a third-grade education, and later from a female high school teacher, who saw the possibilities in Evelyn and encouraged her to pursue a college education. When Evelyn reached high school age, her mother moved her family to Colorado so that Evelyn could attend a large, high-quality high school. She advised her daughter, "Get an education and they can never take it away from you" – a phrase that stuck with Evelyn, a girl who was accustomed to having nothing for others to take away.[148]

Sex discrimination was the name of the game throughout Evelyn's years in higher education. In the 1930s, for the most part, women just didn't go to college. If they did, they either attended a teacher's college (which was what Evelyn initially intended to do, until a teacher of hers encouraged her to aim higher), or they majored in home economics. In fact, most women of that era were warned that excessive thought, reading, and other intellectual pursuits would result in mental illness, and that remaining in the domestic sphere would protect them from psychological disturbance. Bucking the conventional wisdom of the era, Evelyn did in fact earn a college degree (and worked as a housekeeper to supplement her scholarship money) and later completed a master's degree at the University of Colorado. Like so many women, unfortunately, she hit the glass ceiling of academia; Evelyn was denied admission to the Ph.D. program at Yale University simply because she was a woman. She was, however, accepted to the program at Johns Hopkins, where she completed her Ph.D. in 1932.[149]

Had she completed her degree and been in the job market during any other time period in history, Evelyn Hooker's professional interests would likely have gone down a completely different path. Her master's level work focused on vicarious learning in rats, and her dissertation topic was discrimination training[150] (the Skinnerian, operant conditioning form of "discrimination training," not the consciousness-raising diversity seminars offered in corporate and educational environments). So how did she make the unlikely shift from Skinner and behaviorism to homosexuality? Simply put, she got sick, and she couldn't find a stable job. Both of these events contributed significantly to the radical detour her career took.

Evelyn completed her Ph.D. requirements at the height of the Great Depression, and at that time there were almost no available positions for newly-minted Ph.D.s. As luck would have it, though, Evelyn obtained

a teaching position at a small women's college near
Baltimore. Two years later, her luck ran out – Evelyn
developed tuberculosis, which was (and still is) a very
deadly illness. She entered a sanitarium in California
and convalesced there for two years. This tuberculosis
"rest cure," while throwing a wrench into her academic
and career path, probably served as the initial turning
point away from her work in Skinnerian psychology. She
got off the academic train, so to speak, and after two
years of reflection and reading, she took a U-turn from
behaviorism to clinical psychology and, after a year of
part-time teaching, accepted a year-long fellowship in
1937 to study clinical psychology in Europe.[151]

The Holocaust (and events leading up to it) is
one of those events in history that completely changed
the way we look at the world and at humanity. In *Man's
Search for Meaning*, Viktor Frankl (himself a Holocaust
survivor) contends that the drive to find meaning in
one's life and in life's events is more powerful than any
other – a theory that undoubtedly helped him make sense
of his own Holocaust experiences.[152] Anyone who lived
through or witnessed the Holocaust was certainly left to
make sense of the nonsensical – and many did so by
using their professional work as a venue for correcting
social injustices. Stanley Milgram, a social psychologist
who was also Jewish, conducted his famous "obedience
study" after witnessing the events of the Holocaust.[153]

Albert Einstein, a German Jew, emigrated to the U.S. as a result of the rise of the Nazi party, and later took action against the Nazis by alerting then-President Franklin D. Roosevelt to the fact that the Germans were likely developing an atomic bomb.[154] Evelyn Hooker, while not Jewish herself, lived with a Jewish family while she completed her fellowship in Germany, and she was profoundly impacted by that experience. In the words of Viktor Frankl, "Between stimulus and response, there is a space. In that space is our power to choose our response. In our response lies our growth and our freedom."[155] Upon her return to the U.S., Evelyn abandoned her own stimulus-response research, and instead chose to live in the space – the space where she could potentially make a difference in the lives of the oppressed.

After returning to the U.S., Evelyn hit the academic glass ceiling once again. She was denied a faculty position in the UCLA psychology department because the department chair couldn't stand the thought of having another woman in the department. As a consolation prize, Evelyn was offered a position at UCLA Extension.[156] Many major universities – including Harvard – have an extension school; these schools, with their open enrollment policies, allow students who would otherwise be unable to attend college to take courses for enrichment, professional advancement, or improvement of basic skills. As a faculty member at an extension school, Evelyn was certainly in the margins of academia, and as such she was more likely to encounter people who lived in the margins of society – including homosexuals.

After teaching at UCLA Extension for several years, Evelyn befriended a gay student who had taken one of her classes, and it was through this friendship that she was introduced to the local gay community. This student urged Evelyn to conduct research with them, and in 1953, she applied to the National Institute of Mental Health (NIMH) for a grant to study the adjustment of homosexual men. Keep in mind that securing government funding to conduct research on homosexuality is nearly impossible, even in 2011. Obtaining an NIMH grant to conduct this type of research in 1953, an era where homosexuals were persecuted, sent to psychiatric hospitals, and given shock treatments, was as likely as jumping off a cliff and expecting to sprout wings. In fact, the chief of the NIMH grants division responded to Evelyn's application in the truest spirit of McCarthyism: "We are prepared to give you the grant, but you may not receive it. Everyone is being investigated. If you don't receive it, you won't know why and we won't know why."[157] Hooker received the grant – some say because of her charm and good looks[158] – and her research continued to be funded until 1961.

In order to assess the adjustment of homosexual men, Hooker chose to compare a group of exclusively homosexual males to a group of exclusively heterosexual males. In the 1950s, it would have been very, very difficult to amass a sample of gay men using typical sampling and recruitment methods. Hooker was studying a group of people who potentially faced serious life consequences if they were publicly identified. Her initial observational studies were conducted through the connections she had made through her former student who was gay, and many of those individuals were associated with a homophile organization called the Mattachine Society (a group which, incidentally, was loosely affiliated with the Communist party and Communist principles). It was through this organization that Hooker was able to find homosexual participants for her study. Interestingly, Hooker had even more difficulty convincing heterosexual men to participate in her study. As Linda Garnets and Douglas Kimmel describe it, Hooker's study became known as "the fairy project,"[159] and no heterosexual man wanted to be seen approaching her office at UCLA, for fear that they would be pegged as "gay by association." She finally got a group of heterosexual men to agree to participate, using her home as a meeting place in order to protect the anonymity of the participants.

To conduct the study, Hooker used three different projective techniques. The first was the Thematic

Apperception Test (TAT), which consists of a series of pictures about which the participant is asked to tell a dramatic story. The second was the Make-a-Picture-Story (MAPS) Test, a measure that is similar to the TAT but involves cutout figures and backgrounds that allow participants to create their own pictures before developing a story. The last was the Rorschach Inkblot Method, in which participants are asked to provide responses to ten ambiguous inkblot images.[160]   Projective tests, which have their origins in psychoanalytic theory, are designed to unearth conflicts, emotions, and personality dynamics that are submerged beneath our conscious awareness. Despite the fact that projective tests have been critiqued for low reliability and validity and rely too heavily on clinical judgment,[161] they were considered to be rigorous psychological measures at the time Hooker's study was conducted.

Both the homosexual and the heterosexual groups were given these three measures, and Hooker presented the sixty unmarked protocols to a team of three expert evaluators, each of whom were tasked with (a) attempting to identify the sexual orientation of each participant, and (b) attempting to differentiate the psychological makeup of the two groups. Hooker didn't want just any expert – she wanted the best of the best. Those turned out to be Bruno Klopfer, one of the foremost experts on the Rorschach; Edwin Shneidman, creator of the MAPS test; and Mortimer Meyer, who scored the TAT protocols.[162] Although several of the homosexual participants essentially "outed" themselves on the MAPS and the TAT by injecting homosexual content into their stories, the Rorschach protocols of the two groups were indistinguishable – it was impossible to determine who was gay and who was straight, and there were no differences between the two groups in terms of psychological adjustment. The MAPS and the TAT protocols of the two groups were equally indistinguishable – again, no differences in adjustment were detected between the homosexual and the heterosexual group.[163] Hooker commented later, "After all, if Bruno Klopfer couldn't tell who was homosexual on the Rorschach, who could?"[164]

Hooker initially presented the results at the 1955 American Psychological Association convention in Chicago, and subsequently published her paper in the *Journal of Projective Techniques* in 1957. With the publication of "The Adjustment of the Male Overt Homosexual," Hooker became known as the first "activist researcher" on behalf of the gay and lesbian community. Supporters referred to her as the "Rosa Parks of the gay rights movement," and activists for and against gay rights both agree that her research was crucial in normalizing and decriminalizing homosexuality. Eight years after her study was published, she was appointed the chair of the newly-established NIMH Task Force on Homosexuality. Their report, which was issued in 1969 (the year that, coincidentally, the Stonewall Riots took place), concluded that homosexuality is a normal variant of the human sexual experience, and that any suffering that homosexuals experience is due to the effects of societal prejudice.[165] Four years later, in 1973, the American Psychiatric Association voted to remove the diagnosis of homosexuality from the Diagnostic and Statistical Manual of Mental Disorders (DSM).[166] Their decision was based largely on Hooker's pioneering research, in conjunction with changing societal attitudes regarding homosexuality. Shortly before her death, Hooker was awarded the 1991 Award for Distinguished Contribution to Psychology in the Public Interest – one of the most prestigious awards to be granted by the APA. The citation on the award read, "Her pioneering study, published in 1957 ... provided empirical evidence that normal homosexuals existed, and supported the radical idea then emerging that homosexuality is within the normal range of human behavior."[167] It's probably fair to say that her work is the reason why that radical idea has since turned mainstream.

———

And yet, how mainstream (and unbiased) is that

perspective? While Hooker's work has been embraced
by the gay community, anti-gay activists see something
much more sinister going on. Hooker, in their view, was
merely a puppet manipulated by gay rights activists – an
academic ingénue who was initiated into the cult of gay
activism in order to advance their agenda. Moreover,
the decision to remove the diagnosis of homosexuality
from the DSM occurred because the APA kowtowed
to political pressures, not because scientific evidence
proved unequivocally that homosexuals were normal.
In fact, critics contend that the flaws in Hooker's study
reveal her political leanings more than anything else.[168]

Are criticisms about these flaws legitimate? The
first criticism involved what is referred to as sampling
bias – a systematic error that can result in some members
of the population being less likely to be included than
others. Hooker didn't recruit participants from the general
population – she specifically contacted the Mattachine
Society, whose members might be more comfortable
and happy with their homosexuality than those in the
general population. Hooker was also accused of drawing
participants from an organization that might have had
a political agenda invested in her research – according
to one account, "the Mattachine Society members
convinced Hooker to embark on a research study of
homosexuality on their behalf in order to advance the
movement."[169] In defense of Hooker, as noted earlier,

probability sampling of homosexuals (which would have ensured that all homosexuals would have had a chance of being selected for the study) would have been impossible in the 1950s, given the cultural hostilities directed towards homosexuals. And yet, it's fair to say that individuals who chose to join the Mattachine Society probably weren't representative of the gay male population.

A second criticism that was levied against Hooker is that her paper appeared in what is referred to as a "second-tier journal." In the field of psychology (and in other academic and professional fields), some journals are more mainstream and prestigious than others. Clinical psychologists, for example, strive for a publication in the *Journal of Consulting and Clinical Psychology*. Developmental psychologists try to get their work published in – you guessed it – *Developmental Psychology*. An article in the *American Psychologist* – the journal that all members of the American Psychological Association receive – is a major feather in one's cap. And, with very few exceptions, rarely do LGBT researchers get their work published in these journals, even in this day and age. That leaves researchers who study sexual orientation to publish their findings in "second-tier" journals, which tend to be more specialized and attract a more limited readership. These include the *Journal of Homosexuality*, *Women and Therapy*, *Journal of GLBT Family Studies*, *Journal of LGBT Health Research*, and *Journal of Lesbian Studies*. Because these journals focus specifically on LGBT issues, it is much easier to get research on LGBT issues published in them. Unfortunately, research manuscripts published in these journals aren't always taken very seriously. That was the case with Hooker's research. In 1957, editors of top-tier psychology journals wouldn't have touched Hooker's paper with a ten-foot pole – and her credentials as a faculty member at an extension school probably wouldn't have pulled any rank with these editors either. That left a second-tier journal as the only option, an unfortunate catch-22 for researchers who study politically charged topics. And, while things have changed to some degree, the academic landscape for LGBT researchers remains largely the same today.

There is a third criticism that was launched against Hooker's research that is, admittedly, harder to explain away. When Hooker was amassing her sample, she chose to eliminate homosexual and heterosexual individuals who were in therapy, or who exhibited "evidence of considerable disturbance."[170] Hooker provided no explanation in her paper as to why she chose to eliminate these individuals. The decision to eliminate these subjects from the sample is the source of the most venomous attacks against Hooker's research, and Hooker was accused of manipulating the study to generate the outcome she was looking for. According to Jeffrey Satinover, "[Hooker] deliberately had her associates recruit participants to obtain a pool of subjects who understood what the 'experiment' was about and how it was to be used to achieve a political goal in transforming society. As she wrote many years later, 'I knew the men for whom the ratings were made, and I was certain as a clinician that they were relatively free from psychopathology.' In other words, she lacked a random sample and tinkered with the composition of both groups."[171] Another source alleges that "Hooker's work itself, however, was the product of a deliberate effort by homosexual activists to bring forward particular, pre-arranged outcomes, an approach that precludes scientific objectivity."[172] Being accused of this kind of bias is a very serious charge – and it was this issue that created skepticism about Hooker's political motives. It also foreshadowed a more serious concern held by anti-gay activists – if Evelyn Hooker could be indoctrinated by the gay activists, then so could the APA.

So was the decision to remove the diagnosis of homosexuality from the DSM based primarily on objective scientific evidence? Or was it engineered by non-scientist gay activists? The chain of events leading to the APA decision began in 1970, when an activist infiltrated the annual APA meeting in San Francisco and disrupted Irving Bieber's session on homosexuality and transsexualism.[173] From that point forward, activists (including the Gay Liberation Front) made their way to the Committee on Nomenclature and Statistics, which was the decision-making body regarding the DSM, and pressured the APA to change their diagnostic classification. At the time, several APA members in high places were sympathetic to the gay activists. Judd Marmor, the APA vice-president, had served with Evelyn Hooker on the NIMH Task Force on Homosexuality. Robert Spitzer, a consultant to the committee, was a sympathizer on civil rights grounds. And the president of the APA was allegedly a closeted homosexual himself.[174] A meeting was arranged between the Committee, outside activists, and gay psychiatrists and psychologists. Charles Silverstein (who is the author of *The Joy of Gay Sex* and *The New Joy of Gay Sex*) presented the case, leading off with Hooker's research. Two-thirds of the APA Board of Trustees voted to remove homosexuality as a psychiatric disorder. Following this decision, the APA issued the following statement in December of 1973:

> Whereas homosexuality in and of itself implies no impairment in judgment, stability, reliability, or vocational capacities, therefore be it resolved, that the American Psychiatric Association deplores all public and private discrimination against homosexuals in such areas as employment, housing, public accommodation, and licensing, and declares that no burden of proof of such judgment, capacity, or reliability

should be placed upon homosexuals greater than that imposed on any other persons. Further, the APA supports and urges the enactment of civil rights legislation at local, state, and federal levels that would insure homosexual citizens the same protections now guaranteed to others. Further, the APA supports and urges the repeal of all legislation making criminal offenses of sexual acts performed by consenting adults in private.[175]

The American Psychological Association, the larger (and less conservative) of the two APAs, passed a similar resolution in 1975.[176] From that point forward, a cascade of cultural change has taken place. Sodomy statutes have been overturned throughout the United States. Various civil rights protections have been granted by states and municipalities to gays and lesbians. And the constitutionality of gay marriage is being debated as we speak.

A few psychiatrists, including Irving Bieber and Charles Socarides, were fiercely opposed to the APA's decision, and were visibly disturbed by the subsequent political statement issued by the Board. Hoping to overturn the decision, they petitioned for a vote on the issue by the APA membership. The membership voted in 1974 to ratify the decision – although a political compromise was reached in order to appease those who still embraced the notion of homosexuality-as-pathology. That same year, the term "Sexual Orientation Disturbance" (later to be termed *ego-dystonic homosexuality*) was introduced into the DSM. This new diagnosis required that individuals with homosexual tendencies experience significant distress as a result of their same-sex attractions. In 1986, largely because some form of dysphoria is common in the initial stages of coming out, all diagnoses involving homosexuality were completely removed from the DSM. Despite these changes, the homosexuality-as-pathology perspective still lives on, its believers charging that the science that has been used to win civil rights for gays and lesbians is biased and flawed.

―――――――――

Is it possible for science to be completely objective? Can the people behind the science be free from their own personal biases? Looking at the advocates in favor of the "homosexuality-as-pathology" perspective paints a very interesting picture. Irving Bieber's *Homosexuality: A Psychoanalytic Study of Male Homosexuals*, a counter-reaction to the 1948 Kinsey Report that characterized the "overinvolved mother/passive-absent father" family dynamic as the major cause of male homosexuality, has been criticized for studying only those homosexuals who were in analytic treatment (ironically, the opposite of what Hooker was charged with in her research). Charles

Socarides, who fought virulently throughout his career against the APA decision, has a son who is openly gay (and who served as Bill Clinton's advisor on gay and lesbian issues, and is currently the executive director for Equality Matters).[177] George Rekers, a psychologist, NARTH supporter, and founder of the Family Research Council (a Christian-based anti-gay organization), was, in 2010, caught in public with a male prostitute, inviting questions about his own sexual leanings.[178] Can we trust the "objectivity" and the agenda of these scientists? Or does "activist research" only swing in one direction?

9

GOLDEN BOY

Although Evelyn Hooker's research had a significant impact on the perception of homosexuality in psychology and mental health, it would be at least three more decades before psychological research on LGBT issues gained any momentum. Part of that momentum coincided with the death of Wayne Placek, who was one of Hooker's gay research participants. Out of gratitude for Hooker's research and her commitment to the gay community, Placek had bequeathed part of his estate to Hooker with the stipulation that it be used to "increase the general public's understanding of homosexuality and to alleviate the stress that gay men and lesbians experience in this and future civilizations."[179] Prior to the creation of this fund, almost no consistent funding sources existed for research on LGBT issues. Gregory Herek, a research psychologist at the University of California at Davis, worked with Hooker in her last years to establish the Wayne F. Placek Fund, and from 1995 to 2007 he chaired the award competition.[180] And, if Evelyn Hooker was "the mother of the homosexual movement," it's probably fair to say that Gregory Herek is Hooker's golden child (and probably the golden child of the LGBT psychological community as well).

Herek has conducted extensive research on prejudice against lesbians and gay men, anti-gay violence, and AIDS-related stigma. He has received over $5 million in federal and state grants to fund his research on gay-related issues – an amount virtually unattainable by most LGBT researchers. Herek also sat on a peer-review panel for the National Institute of Mental Health (NIMH), and he has also reviewed research proposals for the National Science Foundation. For a researcher whose work would have been considered "radical" by most traditional funding agencies, Herek's presence is phenomenal. What has placed him on the LGBT research map, however, has been his social and public policy work, much of it through the American Psychological Association (APA). The list is impressive: he has chaired the APA Committee on Lesbian and Gay Concerns, he served on the APA Task Force on Avoiding Heterosexist Bias in Research, and he also participated on the APA Task Force on AIDS. He has testified before the U.S. legislature on behalf of the APA on issues such as hate crimes, gays and the military, antigay violence, and, more recently, same-sex marriage. He also has assisted the APA in preparing amicus briefs in federal and state Supreme Court cases, involving issues such as sodomy, military policies, same-sex marriage, and the Boy Scouts. He participated in, under the Clinton administration, the 1997 White House Conference on Hate Crimes.[181] The list goes on and on. And it is this work – his social and public policy efforts – that has earned him the moniker of "activist researcher."

To be sure, Herek is in good company – many researchers have followed in Hooker's footsteps and used psychological research to advocate for LGBT rights. And most of them are either lovingly or tauntingly referred to as "activist researchers" as well. Dean Hamer, Charlotte Patterson, Ritch Savin-Williams, Nanette Gartrell, Esther Rothblum, Simon LeVay – depending on one's perspective, all of them have either been celebrated for their support of the LGBT community, or they have been accused of conducting research in order to further the "gay agenda." So, the question is this: is it appropriate to utilize research to further a social goal?

Any college-level research methods textbook will outline the four main purposes of psychological research. Sometimes research is conducted purely for descriptive purposes – for example, a researcher might want to observe and document infant facial expressions in response to a stimulus. Other research studies seek to predict future events, such as whether or not a person with depression is likely to attempt suicide, or whether a marriage will succeed. Still other studies investigate cause and effect, such as whether playing violent video games causes aggression in children and teenagers. A fourth area, applied research, is the area of interest here – research that is used to change people's lives for the better.[182] It is this type of research that is so often referred to as "activist research." And yet, the use of psychological research in public policy can be traced back to *Brown v. Board of Education*, which relied in part on the work of Kenneth and Mamie Phipps Clark to rule that racial segregation in public schools was unconstitutional.[182] In fact, the American Psychological Association testifies before the legislature on a wide range of issues, so that legislators can make informed decisions about issues that affect their constituents. Without testimony and research, legislators and judges might be more likely to make decisions based on public opinion (which can be based on misinformation), rather than on sound science.

Although Gregory Herek has been called an "activist researcher" by groups such as NARTH, he doesn't fit the visual stereotype of a gay activist. In fact, despite the provocative and political nature of his work,

Gregory Herek is very unassuming in appearance and demeanor. His writing, although it lacks panache, is painstakingly detailed, clear, and thorough. He doesn't stage rebellions or engage in any type of incendiary acts. Aside from the subject matter of his research, Herek is a pretty mainstream activist, in that he works within the established system to manifest change. He publishes articles in mainstream APA journals, secures grants from major government funding sources, and participates in the legislative and judicial system by testifying and writing briefs. No other LGBT researcher has been as successful as Herek in operating within the mainstream system to effect change. And Herek's success as an activist picked up where Hooker left off – with a focus on sexual prejudice.

———————

Herek is the go-to guy when it comes to research on homophobia. He has conducted numerous studies involving attitudes towards lesbians and gay men, and in doing so he has attempted to better understand the psychology behind homophobia. And yet, despite the fact that so much of Herek's research has revolved around the popular notion of homophobia, Herek dislikes that term. Why? (As an aside, I am struck by the fact that many people would just go ahead and use a new term, or just briefly explain why that word was chosen. Not Herek. In his characteristically careful and methodical manner, Herek meticulously presents his rationale behind a new phraseology.)

The term *homophobia* conveys an image of a homophobic person – someone like the retired Marine Corps colonel from the film *American Beauty*, a vitriolic homophobe who, we later find out, is desperately defending against his own homosexuality. Or we might visualize someone who displays his homophobia in a more subtle way. He might stumble over the words "lesbian" or "gay," or he might become anxious if a gay person sits next to him. She might buy into outdated "one must be the man, one must be the woman" stereotypes, and laugh nervously at homophobic jokes so she doesn't get called names or be laughed at. In all of these cases, the term homophobia conjures up images of an individual – and that is where the problem lies, argues Herek. Homophobia isn't a fear that can be treated using Pavlovian behavior therapy. It isn't an individual shortcoming – it is a social pathology.[184]

The term *heterosexism* addresses in part the issue of social pathology. Analogous to racism and sexism, heterosexism has two dimensions. On the one hand, it involves the presumption that opposite-sex relationships are the only legitimate form of intimacy. Bans on same-sex marriage or civil unions can be seen as a form of heterosexism. So can the existence of sodomy laws. On the other hand, heterosexism is also a failure to account for the existence of gay, lesbian and bisexual people. It renders gay and lesbian people invisible. When the U.S. military adopted its "don't ask, don't tell" policy, it essentially was reinforcing heterosexist invisibility of gay and lesbian people.

Technically, the term homophobia refers to individual attitudes, whereas heterosexism describes societal-level ideologies. In reality, though, we can't always untangle the personal from the social and institutional. For example, did Proposition 8 pass in California because of homophobic people, or because of heterosexist belief systems? The answer is unclear. Herek proposes a solution in the form of a new vernacular – *sexual prejudice*, which conflates homophobia and heterosexism into one unifying concept. Sexual prejudice refers to all negative attitudes, individual and societal, based on sexual orientation. These attitudes are directed at a social group and its members, and they invoke dislike and/or hostility. And some people are more likely to harbor sexual prejudice than others.[185]

———————

When I think of someone who is prejudiced against lesbians and gay men, a vivid visual stereotype immediately comes to mind. He is an older white man. He has a high school diploma. He's voted Republican since Eisenhower was elected. He goes to church every Sunday. He lives in Alabama – or maybe Georgia, or Arkansas. Or maybe he lives in a rural part of California. He expects his wife to have dinner on the table when he gets home from work. He sees himself as "the man of the house" and demands respect from his family.

Of course, this is a stereotype – not all white men who possess these characteristics engage in sexual prejudice. However, heterosexuals' attitudes towards lesbians and gays are strongly associated with religiosity, political ideology, attitudes about family and gender roles, and the extent and quality of interpersonal contact with lesbians and gay men. More specifically, people with sexual prejudice tend to be older men who are less educated living in less tolerant parts of the country (such as the Midwest or the South). They are more likely to be politically conservative and practice a more fundamentalist religion. They tend to be authoritarian, valuing obedience to and respect for the person or entity in charge. They support traditional gender roles, and they are less sexually permissive – for example, they would be less likely to support sexual activity outside of marriage. They believe that a homosexual orientation is freely chosen. They also – and this appears to be a key factor towards change – tend not to have close friends or family members who are openly gay.[186]

This last point – the lack of contact with gays and lesbians – prompted Herek to investigate the validity of the *contact hypothesis*. Usually applied to racism, the contact hypothesis suggests that, under the right conditions, contact between members of majority and minority groups can reduce prejudice against the minority group. In other words, if our hypothetical homophobe were to have significant contact with a gay person he cared about, such as a brother, son, or friend, he would be more likely to have more positive attitudes about lesbians and gay men in general. And, in fact, in a national opinion survey he conducted with John Capitano, Herek found exactly that. But contact in and of itself wasn't enough – it had to be contact with close friends or immediate family members, and that contact had to involve some discussion about the person's sexual orientation.[187]

So, of course, coming out can reduce sexual prejudice, but sometimes at a cost. Coming out is not always a positive experience. Families still disown their gay and lesbian children, employers still fire (or refuse to hire) gay and lesbian employees, and gay men and lesbians are still victims of verbal and physical assaults. Discrimination is a reality, and gay and lesbian people are well aware of this when they prepare to come out. Not surprisingly, most gay and lesbian people choose first to tell people who would be most receptive to it, and then perhaps come out to people who might be less tolerant. And yet, even with the risks of discrimination, coming out exerts a very powerful influence against homophobia. Nowhere else in American society is this more clear than in the U.S. military, an institution which, until recently, prohibited openly gay and lesbian people from serving – and where the opportunity to test out the contact hypothesis was, due to "don't ask, don't tell," virtually nonexistent.

It was the ubiquitous debate regarding gays in the military that first brought Herek into the public policy spotlight. Opposition to gays serving in the U.S. military dates back at least to 1778, when Lieutenant Gotthold Frederick Enslin became the first soldier to be drummed out of the Continental Army for sodomy.[188] Purging homosexuality from the military peaked during World War II, when psychiatric screening became a part of the induction process, and when homosexuality was viewed as a psychiatric disturbance.[189] However, adherence to restrictions against homosexuals volleyed depending on whether there was a need for more troops. Dovetailing with the various social movements of the 1960s and 1970s, civil rights efforts supporting gays in the military began to emerge, continuing to gain momentum after the 1981 DOD policy banning gays in the military took effect. All of this set the stage for "don't ask, don't tell" - the recently-repealed policy utilized by all branches of the U.S. military.

In 1992, legislation to overturn the ban was introduced in Congress. During his campaign for the presidency, Bill Clinton had promised to allow all citizens to serve openly in the military, regardless of their sexual orientation. Upon being sworn into office, Clinton drafted a proposal lifting the ban, which was met with intense opposition from the public and from varying segments of the federal government. In response to the flood of resistance, Clinton backed off of his campaign promise and reached a compromise with Congress. This compromise took the form of "Don't Ask, Don't Tell, Don't Pursue." Under its terms, military personnel would not be asked about their sexual orientation and would not be discharged simply for being gay. Engaging in sexual conduct with a member of the same sex, however, would still constitute grounds for discharge.[190]

Before talking about Herek's involvement in this issue, it's important to understand the virulent opposition to gays serving in the military. In the Summary Report of the Military Working Group on Recommended Department of Defense Homosexual Policy, one of the biggest issues cited was that of unit cohesion – the idea that homosexuality would threaten the bonding and "singleness of purpose" required for effective military leadership, and that more energy would be directed towards managing internal discord than towards training for combat. More specifically, the Working Group listed the following concerns:

- An "open homosexual" would have difficulty exercising authority as a leader.

- Conflicts would arise over moral and ethical beliefs.

- Allowing open homosexuals to serve would cripple recruitment and retention, because many people wouldn't want to serve alongside gay people.

- Active homosexuals could spread AIDS within the unit.[191]

The Working Group closes by stating that, if gays were allowed to serve in the military, the "core values" of the military profession would change fundamentally. Thus, ALL homosexuality is incompatible with military service – even if homosexuality is closeted.[192]

This is where Herek's involvement begins. As a social psychologist, and as someone who has research expertise on sexual prejudice, Herek was in a unique position to provide informed commentary on this issue.

His first step was to disentangle the "unit cohesion" argument, where he shifted the focus from homosexuals to the homophobic (or the sexually prejudiced, to use Herek's term):

> In essence, the Pentagon's rationale is that heterosexual personnel have such antipathy for gay people that they would be unable and unwilling to serve with them. Moreover, the Department of Defense believes that it is powerless to prevent this hostility from interfering with the military mission. *Thus, the presumed focus of the problem is not really homosexual personnel. Rather, it is heterosexual servicemembers and military leadership* (emphasis added).[193]

What are we really talking about when we refer to "unit cohesion"? My father belonged to a prestigious country club, and periodically our family would go there for dinners and events. As a teenager, I loved going to the club – particularly because I could hang out at the pool and have lunch on my father's tab. However, once I got to college, I started to become more aware of social and political injustices, and I began to question why women, people of color, and Jewish people weren't allowed access to this privileged venue. (I hadn't even really thought about gay people at the time.) I started to see that my family was essentially practicing passive discrimination by being members of this club, and I refused to set foot in that club again. As you might imagine, my father wasn't very happy about this – I'm sure he thought I was being radical and crazy. In effect, I disrupted the "unit cohesion" of my family, because I wasn't willing to participate in discrimination. If I were really "radical and crazy," I could have taken action and disrupted the "unit cohesion" of the club. I chose not to do that.

Is this the same thing? If unit cohesion in the military were disrupted, would it be solely because of the presence of gay people? Are LGBT people merely creating personal conflict within a military unit, or are they challenging the very foundation of an institution? The reality is that the presence of openly gay people in the military would shine an uncomfortable spotlight on sexism and sexual prejudice. Of course, the Department of Defense never intended to address homophobia within its ranks. In fact, the agency made very clear during the DADT era that its "don't ask, don't tell" education package is not a "sensitivity training" workshop intended to eliminate homophobia – its sole purpose is to inform military personnel about their policies.[194] It's easier to eliminate the homosexuals than to address homophobia.

So is the goal to improve cohesion, or to preserve tradition? Let's give the military the benefit of the doubt.

According to Herek, if the true goal is to improve cohesion, then it is important to distinguish between two types of cohesion. Social cohesion refers to the nature and quality of the emotional bonds of friendship, liking, caring, and closeness among group members. A group displays high social cohesion to the extent that its members like each other, prefer to spend their social time together, enjoy each other's company, and feel emotionally close to one another. Task cohesion refers to the shared commitment among members to achieving a goal that requires the collective efforts of the group. A group with high task cohesion is composed of members who share a common goal and who are motivated to coordinate their efforts as a team to achieve that goal. According to Herek, it is the latter – task cohesion – that has the strongest influence on group performance.[195]

As any Introduction to Psychology textbook would indicate, this conclusion is not surprising. Forty years before "don't ask, don't tell" was implemented, a similar insight was made in the form of the now-classic Robbers Cave study, conducted by Muzafer and Carolyn Sherif. They brought 22 11- to 12-year-old boys to a summer camp and randomly assigned them to one of two groups, the Eagles and the Rattlers. At the beginning of the experiment, activities were structured to create a sense of "in-group identity" – team spirit and loyalty, if you will. Then the researchers put the Eagles and

Rattlers in competition for prizes, sparking a fierce rivalry between the two groups. Before long, the Eagles were as antagonistic towards the Rattlers (and vice versa) as die-hard Red Sox fans are to someone who is openly rooting for the Yankees at Fenway Park. (Having been a Yankee fan all my life, I know that these rivalries don't die easily.) And yet, the point of the study was to do exactly that – to make peace between the Eagles and Rattlers. The key was to create a *supraordinate goal* – goals that are achieved through cooperation and interdependence. Believe it or not, the rivalries dissipated, as reaching their goals became more important than harboring hostilities.[196] Certainly sounds like task cohesion to me.

And yet, according to Herek, task cohesion and social cohesion are related. In fact, social cohesion might even be *improved* by task cohesion. The Eagles and the Rattlers, while working towards their common goals, set their prejudices aside and grew to like each other – in this case, task cohesion led to social cohesion. Of course, this experiment only lasted a few weeks – these were relatively short-term rivalries, compared to the long history of sexual prejudice in the military. Yet if the federal government took a stand against sexual prejudice and implemented clear nondiscrimination policies, social cohesion would improve greatly – and sexual prejudice would dissipate. In his 1993 Congressional testimony on behalf of the APA, Herek stated, "Ongoing interpersonal contact in a supportive environment where common goals are emphasized and prejudice is clearly unacceptable is likely to foster positive feelings toward gay men and lesbians."[197]

Dr. Herek offered five principal recommendations to the military for implementing a nondiscriminatory policy:

1. Establish clear norms that sexual orientation is irrelevant to performing one's duty and that everyone should be judged on her or his own merits.

2. Eliminate false stereotypes about gay men and lesbians through education and sensitivity training for all personnel.

3. Set uniform standards for public conduct that apply equally to heterosexual and homosexual personnel.

4. Deal with sexual harassment as a form of conduct rather than as a characteristic of a class of people. Establish that all sexual harassment is unacceptable, regardless of the genders or sexual orientations of individuals involved.

5. Take a firm and highly publicized stand that violence against gay personnel is unacceptable and will be punished quickly and severely. Attach added penalties to antigay violence perpetrated

by military personnel.[198]

Of course, even though the Don't Ask, Don't Tell Repeal Act was signed by President Obama on December 22, 2010, none of these recommendations have yet been implemented by the U.S. government, and the military still adheres to the 17-year-old "don't ask, don't tell" policy. Eleven years after the DADT policy was adopted, the American Psychological Association passed a resolution opposing this policy. While the resolution itself is rather lengthy, citing numerous research studies supporting the right for openly gay and lesbian people to engage in military service, the following statements within the resolution reflect an underlying issue – whether it is appropriate for professional organization such as the APA to be in the business of engaging in activism:

THEREFORE BE IT RESOLVED that APA reaffirms its opposition to discrimination based on sexual orientation ...

BE IT FURTHER RESOLVED that APA take a leadership role among national organizations in seeking to eliminate discrimination in and by the military based on sexual orientation through federal advocacy and all other appropriate means ...

BE IT FURTHER RESOLVED that APA

reaffirms its strong commitment to removing
the stigma of mental illness that has long
been associated with homosexual and bisexual
behavior and orientations; promoting the health
and well-being of lesbian, gay, and bisexual
adults and youth; eliminating violence against
lesbian, gay, and bisexual service members; and
working to ensure the equality of lesbian, gay,
and bisexual people, both as individuals and
members of committed same-sex relationships,
in such areas as employment, housing, public
accommodation, licensing, parenting, and access
to legal benefits.[199]

Many researchers would agree that scientific
knowledge imposes a moral, ethical, and political
responsibility – that scientists have a duty to take action
if personal or social harm is revealed by their research
findings. The APA's Ethical Principles of Psychologists
and Code of Conduct, for example, contains five
aspirational principles, several of which include working
to protect the rights of the disempowered; practicing
non-discrimination, specifically with respect to "age,
gender, gender identity, race, ethnicity, culture, national
origin, religion, sexual orientation, disability, language,
and socioeconomic status"; and working to prevent

discriminatory activities in others.[200] And yet, some believe that the involvement of the APA (and Herek, more specifically) in social justice and political activism is wholly inappropriate – and accusations in this arena, particularly when it comes to issues regarding sexual orientation, have been fierce. One critic, for example, argues that the:

> APA, like many groups involved in human service delivery, has been seized by political activists who have little regard for science or the democratic process. Since the seventies, the American Psychological Association has lobbied the government, filed court briefs, and engaged in and promoted boycotts on behalf of a host of social-moral causes. These causes have included ERA, unrestricted abortion (including abortion for children without parental notification and consent), sex and racial-ethnic discrimination, and homosexual politics.[201]

Jeffrey Satinover, a member of NARTH and a fierce critic of "advocacy science," suggests that mental health associations such as the APA have been co-opted by gay activists, who misuse science and distort findings to further their political agenda. Yet another critic argues that the use of the terms "homophobia" and "sexual prejudice" "has been increasingly evidenced as being a means of psychological intimidation and mind control used in promoting the 'Homosexual Agenda.'"[202] And, like Evelyn Hooker forty years earlier, Gregory Herek is accused of being the contemporary scientific figurehead of the gay lobby within the APA.

So what exactly is "advocacy science" – and who qualifies as an "activist researcher"? The information made available by NARTH, an organization billed as a clearinghouse for scientific and educational information about homosexuality, slants overwhelmingly in the direction of homosexuality-as-pathology and strongly advocates the use of reorientation therapy. Is this an example of "advocacy science" – but in the opposite direction? Another example of questionable advocacy lies within the Family Research Council, an organization that has made the following statement regarding homosexuality:

> Family Research Council believes that homosexual conduct is harmful to the persons who engage in it and to society at large, and can never be affirmed. It is by definition unnatural, and as such is associated with negative physical and psychological health effects. While the origins of same-sex attractions may be complex, there is no convincing evidence that a homosexual identity is ever something genetic or inborn. We oppose the vigorous efforts of homosexual activists

to demand that homosexuality be accepted as equivalent to heterosexuality in law, in the media, and in schools. Attempts to join two men or two women in "marriage" constitute a radical redefinition and falsification of the institution, and FRC supports state and federal constitutional amendments to prevent such redefinition by courts or legislatures. Sympathy must be extended to those who struggle with unwanted same-sex attractions, and every effort should be made to assist such persons to overcome those attractions, as many already have.[203]

As indicated by its name, the Family *Research* Council (emphasis added) bases its arguments partly on research studies – many of which have been conducted by members of the Council. Are these individuals "activist researchers"?

If the definition of an "activist researcher" is a professional who conducts and interprets research studies as a form of action against a perceived injustice, then Gregory Herek certainly fits the bill. Is that a bad thing? Regardless, Herek's involvement in the public policy sphere certainly didn't end with "Don't Ask, Don't Tell."

10

JUSTIFY MY LOVE

"You can't legislate morality."

-Senator Barry Goldwater (R-AZ), on his opposition to the 1964 Civil Rights Act

One of the reasons Gregory Herek's work has been so powerful in the fight for gay rights is that it suggests a connection between personal attitudes and social policy. Of course, this connection poses somewhat of a chicken-or-the-egg conundrum – it's hard to tell whether public attitudes drive social policy, or whether laws and judicial decisions shape public opinion. Perhaps both are true to some degree. When the 1964 Civil Rights Act was passed, for example, 68% of the public supported the passage of such a law – indicating that a tipping point had been reached.[204] And since the passage of that law, which essentially established a new social norm in our culture, overt racism has become extremely politically incorrect (although it's arguable that racism has just gone underground and become more covert). It's no longer socially acceptable to use the "N" word publicly (we won't talk about rap songs), or to publicly proclaim any affiliation with the KKK, or to tell overtly racist jokes.

The argument that laws and policies can sway public opinion was posed very cogently by Gordon Allport, who authored in 1954 the now-classic text *The Nature of Prejudice*. While Allport made clear that "[t]here is no master key" that can unlock all of the root causes of prejudice, "what we have at our disposal is a ring of keys, each of which opens one gate of understanding."[205] While some of the keys that can help to eliminate prejudice include personal contact and educational programs, it is legislation and public policy, referred to as *stateways*, that truly lead to the tsunami of cultural change.[206] Of course, as evidenced by the 1964 Civil Rights Act, a significant cultural attitude adjustment needs to have already taken place before any policy efforts can be successful – but once that happens, a bandwagon effect sets in: "When the initial work has been done, then the legislation in turn becomes educative. The masses of people do not become converts in advance; rather they are converted by the *fait accompli*. . . . They allow themselves to be re-educated by the new norm that prevails."[207] Allport's work, which was inspired through his work with World War II refugees, continues to have a powerful influence on anti-discrimination efforts.

And yet, how relevant are Allport's ideas to the issue of sexual prejudice? How does the connection between attitudes and public policy play out in the arena of sexual orientation? Let's start by looking at two public policy areas that have changed over time – employment rights (particularly for teachers) and sodomy laws.

————————

Thankfully, I work at an institution that has a clear non-discrimination policy against gay and lesbian individuals. I have always felt that I could talk freely with my colleagues about my personal life or socialize with them, not feeling like I needed to conceal any aspect of my life or my personhood. My college offers domestic partner benefits. They allow me to teach a class about sexual orientation (and to take a sabbatical to write a book on the subject!). I am well aware that I am one of the lucky ones.

A close friend of mine, a teacher at a public high school, is not so lucky. Although she is out to her close colleagues and to her principal, she complies with her own version of "don't ask, don't tell" to the majority of people at her school. She judiciously chooses how strongly to intervene when a student says the ever-popular phrase, "That's so gay!" She doesn't speak up when religiously-oriented activities take place on school grounds. She has not attempted to persuade the human resources department to offer domestic partner benefits. Although an element of her own internalized homophobia may be involved, I'm sure she is well aware of the generally unfavorable attitudes towards gay and lesbian schoolteachers in the U.S. She stays silent because she wants to keep her job.

Of course, there has historically been more support in our culture for gay and lesbian college professors than for gay and lesbian schoolteachers. In 1973, when polled about whether an "admitted homosexual" should be allowed to teach at a college or university, 47% indicated that they should. In 2004, that number jumped to 79%.[208] The K-12 educational environment offers a stark contrast, where being fired because of one's sexual orientation was at one time a common reality. That started to change in the 1970s, when anti-discrimination ordinances were passed in counties in states across the U.S., the first in Dade County, Florida, in 1977.[209] In response to the passage of this ordinance, Anita Bryant launched Save Our Children, a crusade based on the conservative Christian belief that homosexuality is a sin (an abomination), and that homosexuals recruit and molest children. Her campaign sparked in California what became known as the Briggs Initiative, which would have banned gays and lesbians from working in public schools. An unlikely supporter of gay rights came in the form of then-governor Ronald Reagan, who was quoted in an editorial as saying, "Whatever else it is, homosexuality is not a contagious disease like the measles. Prevailing scientific opinion is that an individual's sexuality is determined at a very early age and that a child's teachers do not really influence this."[210] A pretty radical viewpoint for a Republican politician who was preparing to run for President! In 1978, 58.4% of voters opposed the proposition.[211]

Given this social and political climate, it is not surprising that historically attitudes towards gay and lesbian schoolteachers in the U.S. have been pretty unfavorable, although attitudes have been improving. In 1981 (several years after the Briggs Initiative and the Dade County ordinance), a Pew Research Center poll found that 51% of respondents believed that school boards had the right to fire teachers who are known homosexuals. When the same question was asked of poll respondents in 2003, that number dropped down to 33%.[212] Gallup polls conducted from 1976 to 2005 have indicated steadily improving attitudes towards gay and lesbian schoolteachers; in 1976, only 26% believed that gays and lesbians should have the right to be employed as elementary school teachers, whereas in 2005 that number jumped to 54%.[213]

Although there has been improvement in attitudes, let's put this in perspective. According to the same Gallup polls, poll respondents in 1976 were more likely to support gays and lesbians to be employed in sales (69%), to be employed as doctors (43%), to serve as a member of the clergy (35%) and to participate in the *U.S. military* (!) (50%) than they were to support the rights of gay and lesbian schoolteachers.[214] In 2005, support for gay and lesbian schoolteachers has barely edged out support for the rights of clergy (49%).[215] Clearly the damaging beliefs that gay and lesbian teachers negatively influence our children are still widespread. This attitude certainly came through in the recent campaign in support of California's Proposition 8, the anti-same-sex marriage initiative: "Children WILL be taught about gay marriage unless we vote YES on Proposition 8!"[216]

Another litmus test for sexual prejudice lies in the acceptance of homosexual sex, or more specifically, of sodomy laws – laws banning specific types of sexual activity that are more common to gay men. Over the course of 21 years, when asked whether homosexual relations should be legal, the acceptance level has ebbed and flowed depending on the cultural and political landscape. For example, in 1976, respondents were evenly split as to whether homosexual relations between two consenting adults should be legal (43%). In the 1980s, when the AIDS epidemic became widely publicized and the U.S. Supreme Court in *Bowers v. Hardwick* upheld the constitutionality of a Georgia sodomy law, tolerance of homosexual relations dipped to about 35%. Acceptance for gay and lesbian sexual activity slowly increased, peaking throughout the 2000s until 2004, when *Lawrence v. Texas* deemed sodomy laws unconstitutional. That year, acceptance for homosexual activity dipped into the minority, but since then there has been a steady increase of acceptance.[217]

So how do social attitudes translate into public policy decisions? Even though acceptance of gay and lesbian schoolteachers has yet to reach a comfortable majority, their rights have been secured by a number of public policy efforts – in this case, through the voter initiative process. And even though a sizable minority still opposes homosexual sex, sodomy laws have been overturned throughout the United States – not by voters, but by the judicial system. Neither of these policy efforts has resulted in a significant wave of attitude change – a lot of parents would still be uncomfortable with the idea of a gay kindergarten teacher, and many people still squirm at the idea of two men engaging in anal sex. And yet, there haven't been any recent widespread political efforts to remove gay schoolteachers from public schools, nor has any major effort been made to reinstate sodomy laws. Pro-gay attitudes seem to be increasing steadily, but at a very slow pace – not at all the surge of change that Allport would have predicted.

Laws may change attitudes – but Allport failed to predict what would happen when the laws of the land conflict with the word of God. Most major religions practiced around the world view homosexuality as a sin. And while the laws of this constitutional republic have existed for more than two hundred years, the scriptures were written thousands of years ago. For a significant number of people, it's impossible for civil law to trump the word of God. Allport himself said in *The Nature of Prejudice* that "Laws in line with one's conscience are likely to be obeyed."[218] It then becomes a question of where the moral high road lies – with government or with God.

Consider what the Bible has to say about those who teach children. For example, Proverbs 22:6 states, "Train up a child in the way he should go; and when he is old, he will not depart from it." In other words, people who are living an immoral lifestyle cannot effectively teach children how to live a moral life by God's word. Films like *It's Elementary*, intended to teach tolerance and acceptance of homosexuality to children, have been viewed by anti-gay activists as advancing the homosexual agenda in public schools. The Gay, Lesbian, and Straight Education Network (GLSEN), an organization dedicated to improving the school climate for LBGT students, has been accused of going beyond teaching tolerance; their goal, according to anti-gay activists, is "saturation and conversion" of our children – the very thing that the Bible warns us against.

The Bible has plenty more to say about sodomy. Numerous references are made in the Old Testament: In Leviticus 18:22, "Thou shalt not lie with mankind, as with womankind; it is abomination." And this, in Leviticus 20:13: "If a man also lie with mankind, as he lieth with a woman, both of them have committed an abomination: they shall surely be put to death; their blood shall be upon them." Even the New Testament dictates against homosexual relations, at least for men: I Corinthians 6:9-10 states, "Know ye not that the unrighteous shall not inherit the kingdom of God? Be not deceived: neither fornicators, nor idolaters, nor adulterers, nor effeminate, nor abusers of themselves with mankind, nor thieves, nor covetous, nor drunkards, nor revilers, nor extortioners, shall inherit the kingdom of God." According to the Bible, homosexual sex isn't just a garden-variety sin – it is a sin that is punishable by death.

Of course, the issue of marriage inevitably arises. And it's probably no accident that the issue of same-sex marriage eventually ascended into the spotlight.

If homosexual sex is a sin, and if homosexuals are a dangerous influence on our children, then imagine the cultural reaction to the idea of two same-sex adults shacking up and raising their own children. It's no wonder that the issue of same-sex marriage rose up, in tidal wave form, in the wake of these previous issues. And God has certainly entered the equation on this one too.

Nineteen ninety-three was a landmark year. The "Don't Ask, Don't Tell" military policy was instituted in December of that year. Dean Hamer published his famous "gay gene" paper. And, in that same year, the Hawai'i State Supreme court ruled in *Baehr v. Lewin* that it was discriminatory to exclude same-sex couples from marriage.[219]   Opponents to same-sex marriage, fearing that a domino effect was in the works, worked to erect two separate roadblocks to gay marriage, the first of which involved the passage of the 1996 Defense of Marriage Act, signed by then-President Bill Clinton with overwhelming support from both the House and the Senate. The text of this federal law defines marriage as a union between one man and one woman, and it clarifies that no state (or political subdivision in the United States) is obligated to recognize same-sex marriages performed in other states.[220]   While the passage of this law was a crushing blow to supporters of same-sex marriage, it was the second of the two roadblocks that has had a more powerful impact – this being the use of the constitutional amendment process to prohibit same-sex marriage. With the passage of Amendment 2, which granted the state legislature the power to reserve marriage to opposite-sex couples, Hawaii became the first state to put the issue to the voters. Shortly thereafter, other states followed suit, although with a twist – instead of granting the power to define marriage to the legislature, these ballot initiatives involved voter-designed constitutional amendments – thus the second major roadblock to gay marriage. Since then, although many states have enacted bans against same-sex marriage, the initiative that shifted the political landscape on this issue was California's Proposition 8.

Amidst fears that our computer-driven society would collapse on January 1, 2000, the beginnings of the same-sex marriage debate in California were just beginning to take shape. That year, on March 7, Proposition 22 won by a comfortable majority. This one-sentence code, also known as the Knight Initiative, changed the Family Code to define the union of a man and a woman as the only recognizable form of marriage in California.[221] This voter-driven initiative launched a series of efforts in the California legislature to legalize same-sex marriage. Twice, the legislature approved a same-sex marriage bill, and twice Gov. Arnold Schwarzenegger vetoed that bill –

citing the Knight Initiative. Clearly, voters' attitudes had spoken, and attempts to change those attitudes through Allport-style stateways were futile.

Meanwhile, another battle was brewing in the same-sex marriage war, this time in the judicial system. Citing the state constitution's equal protection clause, then-mayor Gavin Newsom of San Francisco issued a directive to the city-county clerk to begin issuing marriage licenses to same-sex couples.[222] From February 12 to March 11, 2004, about 4,000 marriage licenses were issued to same-sex couples. The marriages were halted by the California Supreme Court, and the marriages were voided on August 12, 2004.[223] Embittered by this decision, several couples filed suit against the state, declaring war in the judicial system. A series of appeals brought the case to the California Supreme Court, which, on May 15, 2008, overturned the Knight Initiative, allowing for same-sex couples to get married in California.[224]

Although the lesbian and gay community celebrated victory, opponents to same-sex marriage stepped up their efforts, this time through a proposed constitutional amendment. Proposition 8, which sought to amend the state constitution by defining marriage as between one man and one woman, was placed on that year's general election ballot. This campaign was waged on the national scene, involving out-of-state supporters such as the Mormon church. Supporters of Proposition 8 attempted to incite fear and anger in voters, with images of innocent-looking schoolchildren and statements such as "Gay marriage will be taught in public schools – unless we vote Yes on Proposition 8."[225] One Yes on 8 ad began like this: "Four judges ignored 4 million voters and imposed same-sex marriage on California."[226] Another Yes on 8 commercial featured a gay male couple in an uncomfortable conversation with their young daughter, trying to respond to her earnest questions about where babies come from. After her dads clarify that only mommies have babies, and that you don't have to be married to have a baby, she asks innocently, "Then what's marriage for?" The ad ends with, "Let's not confuse our kids!"[227] Although the Bible was rarely mentioned in political advertising, it was clear that the word of God was the invisible hand.

No on 8 supporters, on the other hand, attempted to win voters over with reason, comparing homophobia to sexism and racism and citing "the law of the land." One ad, featuring Samuel L. Jackson, referenced examples of prejudice and discrimination throughout American (and specifically California) history, including the internment of Japanese-Americans during World War II, housing discrimination against Armenian-Americans, and, in probably the most relevant comparison, the ban on interracial marriages overturned by the 1967 *Loving v. Virginia* Supreme Court decision. The ad, like others encouraging a "no" vote on the initiative, called for the creation of a more tolerant society.[228]

Fear and anger won out over appeal to reason, although only by a slim margin. Proposition 8 passed by 52%.[229] Although California is only but one example, a quick survey of the same-sex marriage issue in other states yields an interesting observation. As of this writing, twenty-nine states have voter-approved constitutional bans against same-sex marriage, while four states, through decisions made by courts and legislatures, allow gay couples to marry (not including Maine), and ten states (including California) confer either a civil union or domestic partnership status for same-sex couples. Clearly voter attitudes have driven public policy, not the other way around.

Since the passage of Proposition 8, a federal lawsuit was filed that challenges the constitutional validity of the decision. Groups such as Equality California and the Courage Campaign seized the opportunity to present two major arguments: that marriage is a fundamental right that should be extended to all citizens; that there are no significant differences between same-sex and opposite-sex relationships that justify a ban on gay marriage; and that legal recognition of relationships bestows a range of benefits to couples (and to their children), including relationship longevity, financial security, and physical and mental health benefits. One of the expert witnesses brought in to make this argument was – you guessed it – Gregory Herek. His level of credibility within the LGBT community and within mainstream research, academic, and government institutions made him the natural choice. Herek had previously participated in writing amicus curiae briefs addressing the constitutionality of laws banning same-sex marriage in five states. He also wrote an article for the *American Psychologist*, the official journal of the American Psychological Association (and the most widely read publication by members of the APA), on the legal recognition of same-sex marriage in the U.S.[230] In his classic punctilious manner, Herek carefully laid out the data, citing work by researchers such as Charlotte Patterson, Nanette Gartrell, Lawrence Kurdek, Leticia Anne Peplau (all of whom have studied lesbian and gay couples extensively) and John Gottman (who is a famous couples therapist and researcher). One hundred forty-eight references in his article led Herek to conclude that same-sex couples are just as normal and mundane as their heterosexual counterparts. More specifically,

> • Although there are some differences between same-sex and opposite-sex relationships (such as level of support from family members and flexibility of gender roles), more similarities than differences exist. Moreover, the differences that

do exist don't appear to justify the ban on same-sex marriage.

• Having same-sex parents isn't at all harmful to children. Studies of gay and lesbian families consistently show that they are just as healthy as heterosexual families. The research also shows that having two parents is better than one, whether parents are heterosexual or homosexual.

• Marriage bestows several benefits, particularly financial and economic security, which often translates into physical and mental health benefits.231

Not surprisingly, despite his meticulous and careful approach, Herek's article (from which his Proposition 8 testimony was drawn) evoked a strong reaction from opponents of same-sex marriage, particularly from organizations such as NARTH, Focus on the Family, and the Family Research Council. Once again, Herek was accused of being an "activist researcher." One respondent to his article called for "a measured approach" to "distinguish the social scientist from the social activist," insinuating that his statements were anything but measured.[232] Another respondent criticized Herek for blurring "the line between science and advocacy."[233] Yet again, we have the issue of science being utilized for social justice purposes.

And it worked. On August 4, 2010, Judge Vaughn Walker, clearly swayed by Herek's testimony (and the testimony of scores of other experts) ruled Proposition 8 unconstitutional. In his ruling, Walker stated the following:

> Proposition 8 fails to advance any rational basis in singling out gay men and lesbians for denial of a marriage license. Because California has no interest in discriminating against gay men and lesbians, and because Proposition 8 prevents California from fulfilling its constitutional obligation to provide marriages on an equal basis, the court concludes that Proposition 8 is unconstitutional.[234]

Throughout the trial, public speculation about the presiding judge's sexual orientation began to arise. A February 7, 2010 article in the *San Francisco Chronicle* described Walker's sexuality as an "open secret."[235] *The New York Times* took up the issue the day after Walker issued his decision.[236] And even though Walker himself didn't publicly come out as gay until April of 2011,[237] immediately after the August 4 ruling Walker was accused of being – surprise! – an "activist judge" with a "gay agenda." Supporters of Proposition 8 filed a motion to vacate Walker's decision, arguing that he should have recused himself due to a conflict of interest; that motion

was denied, and the case appears to be on its way to the
U.S. Supreme Court.

***

Despite the fact that same-sex marriage has
become a significant litmus test for social and political
acceptance of gay and lesbian people, same-sex marriage
is not uniformly supported within the LGBT community
– particularly among radical lesbian feminists. Lesbian
feminists, also known as "political lesbians," were much
more active during the 1970s and 1980s, although some
radical lesbian feminist groups and publications still
exist. Radical lesbian feminists believe that oppression
lies within patriarchy, and that all of our existing cultural
institutions support and reinforce the domination of
men over women. In order to escape this domination
and become empowered, according to radical lesbian
feminists, women need to cut all ties with men and male
privilege and create a female-oriented culture. Marriage,
in any form, is a tool of the patriarchy that straitjackets
women into submission, and having children cinches the
straitjacket even tighter.

Interestingly, their arguments against same-sex
marriage closely mirror those of their conservative
counterparts, although with a twist: both agree that
marriage is the chief building block of civilization (or

at least a patriarchal civilization), although conservatives believe that the institution of marriage needs to be strengthened, whereas the radical lesbian feminists contend that this institution needs to be torn down completely. If same-sex couples gain the right to marry, they only become further assimilated into the world of heterosexual male patriarchy – and radical lesbian feminists believe that assimilation into mainstream culture equals death. To quote one lesbian separatist who was recently interviewed for the *New Yorker*, "Gays in the military and gay marriage? This is what you guys have come up with?"[238]   In their eyes, Gregory Herek is anything but a radical activist – he is a puppet of the patriarchy, using "the master's tools" to help gay and lesbian people gain entry into the most male- and heterosexual-identified institutions in our culture.

While radical lesbian feminism has faded into relative obscurity in recent decades, another group has emerged that poses a threat to the same-sex marriage agenda – this group being the polyamory community. People who are polyamorous engage in intimate love and sexual relationships with more than one person. Polyamorous relationships can take many forms – some people are in triadic relationships, some have one or two primary partners and several secondary partners, and some people form quads (two couples involved with each other). Some polyamorous people live in larger "tribes." Some practice "polyfidelity," in which they are sexual only with members of their triad, quad, or tribe. Others engage in open relationships, giving permission to have sex outside of the relationship. Some relationships are same-gender, others are multiple-gender. Obviously polyamorous relationships are quite diverse – and they don't fit cleanly into the two-person, binary marriage equation.[239]

Although the polyamory community hasn't been visibly politically active in the same-sex marriage debate, they certainly have shown up on the radar screen of both conservative groups and gay marriage advocates. Opponents of same-sex marriage (including the LDS church, which ironically has a colorful history of polygamy) point to the polyamorists in their "slippery slope" argument that legalizing same-sex marriage will open the door to legalizing polyamory and other aberrant relationships. Supporters of same-sex marriage, on the other hand, in trying to prove that their relationships are anything but aberrant, have attempted to distance themselves from the polyamory community, fearing that any association with them will undermine their political goals. As a result, people who practice polyamory have found anything but a safe haven within the LGBT community, and can't count on gay activists to advocate for their rights. Although one large-scale study has indicated that children of poly parents can be quite healthy as long as they're in a stable home with loving parents,[240]   most polyfamilies choose to remain underground, for fear that their children might be taken away from them.[241]

These dissenting voices – and "aberrant" communities – raise some uncomfortable questions. Does dismantling prejudice and oppression rest upon persuading the masses that gay and lesbian people are just like everyone else, and should be allowed to enlist in the military, become a member of the clergy, and get married? Or would laws protecting these "civil rights" only further disempower and oppress non-heterosexuals? Most of the LGBT community's political goals rest on the assumption of normalcy: the belief that homosexuality is not a mental illness; the argument that gays and lesbians can serve our country just like any other U.S. citizen; the contention that same-sex couples argue, pay taxes, and raise children, just like heterosexual couples. And it's the assumption of equality that wins civil rights battles. Of course, Gordon Allport believed that stateways were one of the keys to equality, not a tool of the oppressor. To refer back to Barry Goldwater's famous words, perhaps we can't effectively legislate morality because there isn't a universally agreed-upon moral code. Some believe in a God-dictated code, others adhere to a government-dictated code – and a small but vocal minority believe that neither one will truly bring freedom and salvation.

11

CONCLUSION

How do you end a story that is still being told? Certainly not with a fairy-tale ending, as noted in the introduction of this book (no potentially offensive pun intended). For me, this story ends just like it began – initially, with a blank computer screen and a jumble of thoughts. And yet, somehow I feel like I "should" conclude this book nicely and neatly, wrapping up these ideas in a box with rainbow-colored paper, tied with a shiny pink bow.

There do, however, seem to be some common threads that run through each of these stories, although they might not tie themselves neatly into a bow. Perhaps the clearest one involves the illusion of pure scientific objectivity. Can we separate the scientist from the science, the policy-maker from the policy, the judge from the judgment? The scientific community tries to. Academic journals, in their APA-style citations, reveal only the last names and first initials of the researchers - "LeVay, S.," or "Diamond, L.," or "Bailey, J.M." We learn nothing of the gender, or race, or sexual orientation of these individuals. We learn nothing about what got them interested in their subject matter in the first place. And while scientific conventional wisdom dictates that our human side invokes bias, I believe that the human side matters. It *matters* that Simon LeVay and Dean Hamer are gay, both with their own personal experiences of coming to terms with their sexuality. It *matters* that Lisa Diamond has insider status within the lesbian community, and that her personal experiences didn't fit the existing paradigm. It *matters* that Michael Bailey is a straight white man researching an oppressed class of people. It *matters* that Evelyn Hooker experienced a series of life-changing events that eventually led her to study sexual orientation. Most traditional researchers would argue that all of this is just fluff, distracting us from the essence of scientific truth. At least with respect to psychological research, I think context is essential. Context gives meaning and importance to the findings. And frankly, context is inevitable. Try as we might, we can never fully closet our personalities, our experiences, or our humanness in order to "protect" against bias. Who we are and what we've gone through in life creates the lens through which we view the world. It informs the questions we ask, the data we gather, the interpretations we make. Focusing on our humanness contributes to the research process.

Humans are inherent storytellers. Most people enjoy talking about themselves in one way or another. And researchers are storytellers too – they just tell their stories in a different way. Each study a researcher conducts is like a window into his or her soul. They have a life experience and perspective that they either consciously or unconsciously want to give voice to, and science provides a venue and a language to communicate that experience. Without the human experience, we wouldn't have science. And science adds legitimacy to our stories.

Of course, our humanness always involves a dark side, and part of our humanness involves fear. We are biologically hard-wired to fear. If a car is about to crash into mine, I'm going to experience fear. If a gun is pointed at me, I'm going to experience fear. Both of these are life-and-death fears. Of course, many of our fears are downright neurotic. Some of my crazy and non-life-threatening fears include: being late, screwing up my child, calling someone I don't know, being faced with a large and unexpected expense – just to name a few. We are driven by fear. And I'd argue that some – perhaps many – of our research and policy decisions are driven by fear as well. Religious groups fear that acceptance of gay and lesbian people will tear apart the social and moral fabric of our culture. Gay and lesbian activists fear that failing to secure basic civil rights will result in invisibility, physical and verbal abuse, and possibly even death. Some people with anti-gay sentiments may unconsciously fear their own sexual feelings, for merely acknowledging their own same-sex attractions puts them in an intolerable emotional state. None of these fears are trivial. While some fear actual death, others fear death of the spirit. And many would consider spirit-death to be the far worse of the two.

This fear touches the scientific community too. Some fear that too much talk of "sexual fluidity" will undermine the political gains achieved by using the "born that way" theory. Some fear that too much talk of "autogynephilia" will result in fewer gender reassignment surgeries being performed. Some fear that the newly adopted term "DSD" will once again silence and marginalize individuals who are intersex. And so those researchers who refuse to toe the party line – Lisa Diamond, Michael Bailey, Alice Dreger – are vilified, and in some cases almost literally burned at the stake. Going off-message has powerful consequences, all driven by fear.

None of these fears are unrealistic. However, I do believe they routinely get acted-out upon, rather than being examined and processed. Instead of acknowledging his fear of possibly being gay himself, a man might act out his fear by victimizing other gay men. Instead of examining one's internal reaction to, say, the "autogynephilia" theory, a transgender activist may try to kill the messenger rather than the message (so to speak). Instead of exploring one's discomfort with biological theories of homosexuality, a gay man might publicly label researchers who advocate these theories as "eugenicists" who are trying to cleanse the world of homosexuality. Individuals act out, as do larger groups and organizations – the Westboro Baptist Church, with its "GOD HATES FAGS" signs, is an extreme example of this. Clearly, this acting-out serves a purpose. When we act out, we distract ourselves from uncomfortable, intolerable, painful feelings. When we silence the dissidents and attempt to squeeze people into a politically-correct (but flawed) paradigm, we are invalidating their personal truth. And frankly, I think this brand of distraction is much more dangerous than the "distraction" of subjectivity in research.

If the yin of human nature is based in fear, the yang, I believe, is guided by altruism and social justice. We want to do good in the world. We want to make a difference in people's lives. And psychological research is a powerful vehicle for social change. The multiple detours that both Simon LeVay and Dean Hamer took in their professional careers provide evidence for that. The personal and professional risks Evelyn Hooker was willing to take speak volumes regarding her drive for social justice. The tireless public policy work Gregory Herek has engaged in over the last two decades was done purely for social justice purposes. Alice Dreger, despite the fact that many intersex people don't find her ideas to be helpful at all, appears to sincerely want to advocate for this community. These researchers aren't in it for the money. They don't seem to be in it for fame and celebrity, either. They want people to be treated fairly. They want to make a positive difference in the world. Frankly, that's what "activist research" is all about.

Researchers, for the most part, also want to tell the truth. Lisa Diamond wants to tell the truth about women and sexual fluidity. Milton Diamond wanted to tell the truth about the devastating impact of silencing intersex conditions. Michael Bailey, I believe (despite the sentiments of his antagonists), wants to tell the truth about transpeople. Whether these "truths" are really true is another story. However, I do think that each of these researchers, no matter how unpopular, controversial, or politically incorrect their theories might be, are motivated by integrity. They're willing to incur significant risk in order to convey their sense of the truth. Of course, many people are willing to take a personal or professional hit in order to make their message heard, even if the message is completely inaccurate and crazy. However, there's a huge difference between a fear-based motivation (like what we see in organizations like NARTH, Focus on the Family, and the Family Research Council) and a motivation based on trust and integrity. Fear-based motivation never leads to the truth.

Sometimes the truth is uncomfortable, even painful and scary. But the truths that exist in the LGBTQ community – all of those truths – deserve a voice. And those collective truths will, I think, ultimately lead to social justice.

In the introduction to this book, I suggested that a powerful wisdom lies within the human factor behind the research. If we don't pull back the veil of objectivity and peer more deeply into the backdrop, we lose a vital opportunity to really understand the complex nuances and politics behind sexual orientation issues. I would go so far as to suggest that *all* psychological research – not just sexual orientation research – has a backdrop that can quite possibly teach us more about that subject area than the research studies themselves. And it's the human factor that truly brings meaning to the work.

NOTES

CHAPTER 2 – THE OUT GAY SCIENTIST

[1]Freud, 1957.
[2]Bieber, 1962.
[3]Hooker, 1957.
[4]Bailey, 2003a.
[5]Nimmons, 1994.
[6]Allen & Gorski, 1991; Allen & Gorski, 1992.
[7]Nimmons, 1994.
[8]Bailey & Pillard, 1991.
[9]Blanchard & Sheridan, 1992.
[10]Hamer, 1993.
[11]Socarides, 1995.
[12]Nimmons, 1994.
[13]Transsexual Road Map, n.d.(e).
[14]Byne, 2001.
[15]San Diego Superior Court, 1994.
[16]Lever, 1994; Lever, 1995.
[17]Nimmons, 1994.
[18]Nimmons, 1994.

[19]LeVay, 1997.
[20]Nicolosi, 1997.
[21]Nicolosi, 1997.

CHAPTER 3 – THE VEIL OF OBJECTIVITY

[22]The Kinsey Institute for Research in Sex, Gender, and Reproduction, n.d.
[23]Irvine, 1991.
[24]Hamer, 1994, p. 24.
[25]Hamer, 1994.
[26]"Portrait," 1997.
[27]Hamer, 1994 p. 40.
[28]Pattatucci-Aragon, 2001, p. 4.
[29]Henry, 1993.
[30]Henry, 1993.
[31]Willis, 1993.
[32]Hamer, 1994.
[33]Transsexual Road Map, n.d.(b).
[34]Marshall, 1995.
[35]Hamer, 1994, p. 212.
[36]Hamer, 1999.
[37]Mustanski et al., 2005.
[38]Pattatucci-Aragon, 2001, p. 9.
[39]Pattatucci-Aragon, 2001, p. 8.
[40]Pattatucci-Aragon, 2001, p. 9.
[41]Pattatucci-Aragon, 2001, p. 9.
[42]Pattatucci-Aragon, 2001, p. 9.
[43]"WEDDINGS/CELEBRATIONS," 2004.
[44]Hamer, 2009.

CHAPTER 4 – SUSPICIOUSLY STRAIGHT

[45]Bailey, Willerman, & Parks, 1991.
[46]Bailey, Willerman, & Parks, 1991.
[47]Bailey, 2003b.

[48]Bailey, 2003b.
[49]Bailey, 2003b.
[50]Transsexual Road Map, n.d.(c).
[51]Hamer, 1993.
[52]Greenberg & Bailey, 2001.
[53]Harmon, 2007.
[54]California Cryobank, n.d.
[55]Associated Press, 2005.
[56]Bailey, 2003b, pp. 114-115.
[57]Sailer, 2002.

CHAPTER 5 – SWINGING BOTH WAYS

[58]"Coming out," 2009.
[59]Cass, 1979.
[60]Pilkington & D'Augelli, 1995.
[61]Herek, n.d.(f).
[62]Coleman, 1982.
[63]Troiden, 1989.
[64]McCarn & Fassinger, 1996.
[65]D'Augelli, 1994.
[66]Names and all identifying details have been changed in this vignette.
[67]Savin-Williams & Diamond, 1997.
[68]Diamond, 2008, p. 3.
[69]Diamond, 2008.
[70]Diamond, 2008.
[71]Diamond, 2008.
[72]Diamond, 2008.
[73]Ochs, 1996.
[74]Kinsey, 1948.
[75]Mosher, Chandra, & Jones, 2005.
[76]Savin-Williams, 2005.
[77]Lever, 1994; Lever, 1995.
[78]National Association for Research and Therapy of Homosexuality, n.d.(c).
[79]National Association for Research and Therapy of Homosexuality,

n.d.(a).
[80]Nicolosi, 2009.
[81]Byrd, 2010.
[82]National Association for Research and Therapy of Homosexuality, n.d.(b).
[83]National Association for Research and Therapy of Homosexuality, n.d.(b).
[84]Diamond, 2008.
[85]TruthWinsOut, n.d.
[86]"Dr. Lisa Diamond," 2008.

CHAPTER 6 – GOING OFF-MESSAGE

[87]San Francisco Pride, n.d.
[88]O'Brien, 2007.
[89]Jhally, 1999.
[90]Ducat, 2004.
[91]Bailey, 2003b.
[92]LeVay, 1997.
[93]Bergling, 2001.
[94]Remafedi, Farrow, & Deisher, 1991.
[95]Raymond, 1979.
[96]Raymond, 1979.
[97]Raymond, 1979.
[98]Amazon.com, 2011.
[99]Transsexual Road Map, n.d.(d).
[100]Camp Trans, 2011.
[101]Vogel, 2006.
[102]McHugh, 2009.
[103]Zhou, Hofman, Gooren, & Swaab, 1995.
[104]Transsexual Road Map, n.d.(a); Transgender London, 2010.
[105]Blanchard, 1989.
[106]Blanchard, 1989.
[107]Bailey, 2003b, p. 168.
[108]Bailey, n.d.
[109]Bailey, n.d.
[110]Dreger, 2008.

[111]Dreger, 2008, p. 368.
[112]Dreger, 2008, p. 368.
[113]Dreger, 2008.
[114]Dreger, 2008, p. 368.
[115]Federal Bureau of Investigation, 2008.

CHAPTER 7 – TOPPLING THE TOWER OF BABEL

[116]Bornstein, 1994, p. 8.
[117]Scolar, 2001.
[118]Feinberg, 1999, p. 1.
[119]United States Court of Appeals, Eighth Circuit, 1998.
[120]Hackett, 2000.
[121]Feinberg, 1996.
[122]Intersex Society of North America, n.d.(a).
[123]Colapinto, 2001.
[124]Money, 1973.
[125]Money, 1975.
[126]Money & Tucker, 1975.
[127]Diamond, 1965.
[128]Fausto-Sterling, 2000, p. 70.
[129]BBC TV, 2000; BBC TV, 2004.
[130]Diamond & Sigmundson, 1997.
[131]Colapinto, 2001.
[132]Canadian Press, 2004.
[133]Weil, 2006.
[134]Weil, 2006.
[135]Liu, 1998.
[136]Weil, 2006.
[137]Weil, 2006.
[138]Intersex Society of North America, n.d.(b).
[139]Lee, Houk, Ahmed, & Hughes, 2006.
[140]Intersex Society of North America, n.d.(c).
[141]Intersex Society of North America, n.d.(c).
[142]Accord Alliance, n.d..
[143]Lee, Houk, Ahmed, & Hughes, 2006.
[144]Intersex Society of North America, n.d.(c).

[145]Dreger, 2007.
[146]Oii Australia, n.d.

CHAPTER 8 –
THE FIRST "GAY ACTIVIST" RESEARCHER

[147]Although the term "homosexual" is seen as an outdated and pejorative term in the gay and lesbian community, I chose to retain the use of this term in this chapter, given its historical context.
[148]"Awards for," 1992, p. 502.
[149]Kimmel & Garnets, 2003.
[150]Herek, n.d.(a).
[151]Herek, n.d.(a).
[152]Frankl, 1959.
[153]Blass, 2004.
[154]Dannen, 1998.
[155]Frankl, 1959.
[156]Herek, n.d.(a).
[157]Hooker, 1993, p. 451.
[158]Kimmel & Garnets, 2003, p. 39.
[159]Kimmel & Garnets, 2003, p. 38.
[160]Hooker, 1957.
[161]Wood, Nezworski, Lilienfeld, & Garb, 2003.
[162]Schmiechen, 1992.
[163]Hooker, 1957.
[164]Kimmel & Garnets, 2003.
[165]Herek, n.d.(a).
[166]Herek, n.d.(a).
[167]"Awards for," 1992.
[168]Satinover, n.d.; White, 2007.
[169]White, 2007.
[170]Hooker, 1957.
[171]Satinover, n.d.
[172]White, 2007.
[173]Socarides, 1995.
[174]Glass, 2002.
[175]Bayer, 1981, p. 137.

[176]American Psychological Association, 1975.
[177]Bull, 1999.
[178]Bullock & Thorp, 2010.

CHAPTER 9 – GOLDEN BOY

[179]American Psychological Association, n.d.
[180]American Psychological Association, n.d.
[181]Herek, n.d.(d).
[182]Goodwin, 2009.
[183]United States Supreme Court, 1954; Clark & Clark, 1950.
[184]Herek, n.d.(b).
[185]Herek, n.d.(b).
[186]Herek, 1994.
[187]Herek & Capitano, 1996.
[188]Herek, n.d.(e).
[189]Herek, n.d.(e).
[190]Herek, n.d.(e).
[191]Otjen et al., 1993.
[192]Otjen et al., 1993.
[193]Herek, n.d.(c).
[194]U. S. Department of Defense, 2009.
[195]Herek, 1993.
[196]Sherif, 1958.
[197]Associated Press, 1993.
[198]Associated Press, 1993.
[199]American Psychological Association, 2004.
[200]American Psychological Association, 2010.
[201]Johnson, 1995.
[202]"Homophobia," n.d.
[203]Family Research Council, 2010.

CHAPTER 10 – JUSTIFY MY LOVE

[204]"1964 Civil Rights Act," n.d.
[205]Allport, 1954, p. 208.
[206]Allport, 1954.

[207]Allport, 1954, p. 471.

[208]Herek, n.d.(g).

[209]Pride South Florida, n.d.

[210]Reagan, 1978, p. A19.

[211]Secretary of State, 1978.

[212]Herek, n.d.(g).

[213]Herek, n.d.(g).

[214]Herek, n.d.(g).

[215]Herek, n.d.(g).

[216]ProtectMarriage.com, "Prop 8 ad," 2008.

[217]Herek, n.d.(g).

[218]Allport, 1954, p. 474.

[219]Hawai'i Supreme Court, 1993.

[220]U. S. Government Printing Office, 1996.

[221]California Secretary of State, 2000.

[222]Gordon, 2004.

[223]Supreme Court of California, 2004.

[224]Liptak, 2008.

[225]ProtectMarriage.com, "Yes on 8 TV ad: Everything," 2008.

[226]ProtectMarriage.com, "Yes on 8 TV ad: Whether," 2008.

[227]"Proposition 8 commercial," 2008.

[228]No on 8, 2008.

[229]California Secretary of State, 2008.

[230]Herek. 2006.

[231]Herek, 2006.

[232]Rosik & Byrd, 2007.

[233]Shiller, 2007.

[234]U.S. District Court for the Northern District of California, 2010.

[235]Matier & Ross, 2010.

[236]Schwartz, 2010.

[237]Levine, 2011.

[238]Levy, 2009.

[239]Barker, 2009.

[240]Sheff, in press.

[241]Bennett, 2009.

BIBLIOGRAPHY

Accord Alliance. (n.d.). Our mission. Retrieved from http://
www.accordalliance.org/about/our-mission.html.

Allen, L. S., and Gorski, R. A. (1991). Sexual dimorphism of the anterior commissure and massa in-
termedia of the human brain. *Journal of Comparative
Neurology, 312,* 97-104.

Allen, L.S., and Gorski, R. A. (1992). Sexual orientation
and the size of the anterior commissure of the human
brain. *Proceedings of the National Academy of Sciences, 89,*
7199-7202.

Allport, G. (1954). *The nature of prejudice.* Cambridge, MA:
Addison-Wesley Publishing.

Amazon.com. (2011). Customer reviews: *The transsexual empire: The making of the she-male.* Retrieved from http://
www.amazon.com/Transsexual-Empire-Making-She-
Male-Athene/product-reviews/0807762725/ref=dp_
top_cm_cr_acr_txt?ie=UTF8&showViewpoints=1.

American Psychological Association. (1975). Policy statement on discrimination against homosexuals. *American Psychologist*, *30*, 633.

American Psychological Association. (2004). Sexual orientation and military service. Retrieved from http://www.apa.org/about/governance/council/policy/military.aspx.

American Psychological Association. (2010). Ethical principles of psychologists and code of conduct. Retrieved from http://www.apa.org/ethics/code/index.aspx.

American Psychological Association. (n.d.). Wayne F. Placek Grants. Retrieved from http://www.apa.org/apf/funding/placek.aspx.

Associated Press. (1993, May 5). Psychologist testifies against military's anti-gay ban. Retrieved from http://psychology.ucdavis.edu/rainbow/html/miltest1.html.

Associated Press. (2005, May 5). FDA set to ban gay men as sperm donors. Retrieved from http://www.msnbc.msn.com/id/7749977/.

Awards for distinguished contribution to psychology in the public interest. (1992). *American Psychologist*, *47*, 498-503.

Bailey, J. M. (n.d.). Book controversy question and answer. Retrieved from http://faculty.wcas.northwestern.edu/JMichael-Bailey/controversy.htm.

Bailey, J. M. (2003a). Biological perspectives on sexual orientation. In L. D. Garnets & D. C. Kimmel (Eds.), *Psychological Perspectives on Lesbian, Gay, and Bisexual Experiences* (pp. 50-85). New York: Columbia University Press.

Bailey, J. M. (2003b). *The man who would be queen.* Washington, D. C.: Joseph Henry Press.

Bailey, J. M., Willerman, L., & Parks, C. (1991). A test of the maternal stress theory of human male homosexuality. *Archives of Sexual Behavior, 20*(3), 277-293.

Bailey, J. M., and Pillard, R. C. (1991). A genetic study of male sexual orientation. *Archives of General Psychiatry, 48*, 1089-1096.

Barker, M., and Langdridge, D. (Eds). (2009). *Understanding non-monogamies.* New York: Routledge.

Bayer, R. (1981). *Homosexuality and American psychiatry: The politics of diagnosis.* New York: Basic Books.

BBC TV (Producer). (2000). The boy who was turned into a girl. In *Horizon.* London: BBC TV.

BBC TV (Producer). (2004). Dr. Money and the boy with no penis. In *Horizon.* London: BBC TV.

Bennett, J. (2009, July 29). Only you. And you. And you. *Newsweek.* Retrieved from http://www.newsweek.com/2009/07/28/only-you-and-you-and-you.html.

Bergling, T. (2001). *Sissyphobia: Gay men and effeminate behavior.* Binghamton, NY: Harrington Park Press.

Blanchard, R. (1989). The concept of autogynephilia and the typology of male gender dysphoria. *The Journal of Nervous and Mental Disease*, *177*, 616-623.

Blanchard, R., and Sheridan, P. M. (1992). Sibling size, sibling sex ratio, birth order, and parental age in homosexual and nonhomosexual gender-dysphorics. *Journal of Nervous and Mental Disorders*, *180*, 40-47.

Blass, T. (2004). *The man who shocked the world: The life and legacy of Stanley Milgram*. New York: Basic Books.

Bornstein, K. (1994). *Gender outlaw: On men, women, and the rest of us*. New York: Routledge.

Bull, C. (1999, July 11). His public domain, his private pain. *Washington Post Magazine*.

Bullock, P., & Thorp, B. K. (2010, May 6). Christian right leader George Rekers takes vacation with "rent boy." *Miami NewTimes*. Retrieved from http://www.miaminewtimes.com/2010-05-06/news/christian-right-leader-george-rekers-takes-vacation-with-rent-boy/1/.

Byne, W., Tobet, S., Mattiace, L. A., et al. (2001). The interstitial nuclei of the human anterior hypothalamus: An investigation of variation with sex, sexual orientation, and HIV status. *Hormonal Behavior*, *40*(2), 86-92.

Byrd, A. D. (2010, September 21). Homosexuality: The essentialist argument continues to erode. Retrieved from http://narth.com/2010/09/homosexuality-the-essentialist-argument-continues-to-erode/.

California Secretary of State. (2000). Text of Proposition 22. Retrieved from http://primary2000.sos.ca.gov/VoterGuide/Propositions/22text.htm.

California Secretary of State. (2008, November 4). Statement of vote: November 4, 2008 general election. Retrieved from http://www.sos.ca.gov/elections/sov/2008_general/sov_complete.pdf.

Camp Trans. (2011). Retrieved from http://www.camp-trans.org/.

Canadian Press. (2004, May 12). David Reimer, 38, subject of the John/Joan case. *The New York Times*. Retrieved from http://www.nytimes.com/2004/05/12/us/david-reimer-38-subject-of-the-john-joan-case.html.

Cass, V. C. (1979). Homosexual identity formation: A theoretical model. *Journal of Homosexuality*, *4*(3), 219-235.

Clark, K. B., & Clark, M. P. (1950). Emotional factors in racial identification and preference in Negro children. *The Journal of Negro Education*, *19*(3), 341-350.

Colapinto, J. (2001). *As nature made him. The boy who was raised as a girl*. New York: Perennial.

Coleman, E. (1982). Developmental stages of the coming out process. *Journal of Homosexuality*, *7*(2-3), 31-43.

Coming out. (2009). In *The American Heritage Dictionary of the English Language* (4th edition). New York: Houghton Mifflin.

Dannen, G. (1998). Einstein's letter to Roosevelt, August 2, 1939. Retrieved from http://www.dannen.com/ae-fdr.html.

D'Augelli, A. R. (1994). Identity development and sexual orientation: Toward a model of lesbian, gay, and bisexual development. In A. R. D'Augelli, E. J. Trickett, R. J. Watts, & D. Birman (Eds.), *Human diversity: Perspectives on people in context* (pp. 312-333). San Francisco, CA: Jossey-Bass.

Diamond, L. M. (2008). *Sexual fluidity: Understanding women's love and desire.* Cambridge, MA: Harvard University Press.

Diamond, M. (1965). A critical evaluation of the ontogeny of human sexual behavior. *The Quarterly Review of Biology, 40*(2). Retrieved from http://www.hawaii.edu/PCSS/biblio/articles/1961to1999/1965-critical-evaluation.html.

Diamond, M., & Sigmundson, H. K. (1997). Sex reassignment at birth: Long-term review and clinical implications. *Archives of Pediatric and Adolescent Medicine, 151*(3), 298-304.

Dr. Lisa Diamond: "NARTH distorted my research." (2008). Retrieved from http://www.youtube.com/watch?v=64A2HrvYdYQ.

Dreger, A. D. (2007). Why "disorders of sex development"? (On language and life). Retrieved from http://alicedreger.com/dsd.html.

Dreger, A. D. (2008). The controversy surrounding *The Man Who Would Be Queen*: A case history in the politics of science, identity, and sex in the Internet age. *Archives of Sexual Behavior, 37*, 366-421.

Ducat, S. (2004). *The wimp factor: Gender gaps, holy wars, and the politics of anxious masculinity*. Boston, MA: Beacon Press.

Family Research Council. (n.d.). Human sexuality: Homosexuality. Retrieved from http://www.frc.org/human-sexuality#homosexuality.

Fausto-Sterling, A. (2000). *Sexing the body: Gender politics and the construction of sexuality*. New York: Basic Books.

Federal Bureau of Investigation. (2008). Uniform Crime Reports: Crime in the United States, 2008. Retrieved from http://www2.fbi.gov/ucr/cius2008/index.html.

Feinberg, L. (1996). *Transgender warriors: Making history from Joan of Arc to Dennis Rodman*. Boston, MA: Beacon.

Feinberg, L. (1999). *Trans Liberation: Beyond pink or blue*. Boston, MA: Beacon.

Frankl. V. (1959). *Man's search for meaning*. New York: Pocket Books.

Freud, S. (1957). Letter to an American mother. In Jones, E. (Ed.), *The Life and Work of Sigmund Freud, vol. 3, The*

Last Phase: 1919-1939 (pp. 195-196). New York: Basic Books.

Glass, I. (Producer). (2002, January 18). 81 words. *This American Life*. Chicago, IL: Public Radio International.

Goodwin, C. J. (2009). *Research in psychology: Methods and design* (6th edition). Hoboken, NJ: Wiley.

Gordon, R. (2004, February 11). Newsom's plan for same-sex marriages: Mayor wants to license gay and lesbian couples. *San Francisco Chronicle*. Retrieved from http://www.sfgate.com/cgi-bin/article.cgi?f=/c/a/2004/02/11/MNGRA4U13R1.DTL.

Greenberg, A. and Bailey, J.M. (2001). Parental selection of children's sexual orientation. *Archives of Sexual Behavior, 30*(4), 423-437.

Hackett, T. (2000). The execution of Private Barry Winchell: The real story behind the "don't ask, don't tell" murder. *Rolling Stone*. Retrieved from http://web.archive.org/web/20060213230320/www.davidclemens.com/gaymilitary/rolstobarry.htm.

Hamer, D. H. (1999). Genetics and male sexual orientation. *Science, 285*(5429), 803.

Hamer, D. H. (2009). *Out in the silence*. Retrieved from http://outinthesilence.com/Dean_Hamer.html.

Hamer, D. H., & Copeland, P. (1994). *The science of desire: The search for the gay gene and the biology of behavior*. New York: Simon & Schuster.

Hamer, D. H., Hu, S., Magnuson, V. L., Hu, N., & Pattatucci, A. M. (1993). A linkage between DNA markers on the X chromosome and male sexual orientation. *Science*, *261*(5119), 321-321.

Harmon, A. (2007, May 9). Prenatal test puts Down syndrome in hard focus. *The New York Times*. Retrieved from http://www.nytimes.com/2007/05/09/us/09down.html.

Hawai'i Supreme Court. (1993, May 5). *Baehr v. Lewin*. Retrieved from http://www.danpinello.com/Baehr.htm.

Henry, W. H. (1993, July 26). Born gay? *Time*. Retrieved from http://www.time.com/time/magazine/article/0,9171,978923-3,00.html.

Herek, G. M. (1993). Sexual orientation and military service: A social science perspective. *American Psychologist*, *48*(5), 538-549.

Herek, G. M. (1994). Assessing heterosexuals' attitudes toward lesbians and gay men: A review of empirical research with the ATLG scale. In B. Greene & G. M. Herek (Eds.), *Lesbian and Gay Psychology* (pp. 206-228). Thousand Oaks: Sage Publications.

Herek, G. M. (2006). Legal recognition of same-sex relationships in the United States: A social science perspective.*American Psychologist*, *61*, 607–621

Herek, G. M. (n.d.[a]). Evelyn Hooker: In memoriam. Retrieved from http://psychology.ucdavis.edu/rainbow/html/hooker2.html.

Herek, G. M. (n.d.[b]). Definitions: Homophobia, hetero-sexism, and sexual prejudice. Retrieved from http://psychology.ucdavis.edu/rainbow/html/prej_defn.html.

Herek, G. M. (n.d.[c]). "Don't ask, don't tell" revisited. Retrieved from http://psychology.ucdavis.edu/rainbow/html/military.html.

Herek, G. M. (n.d.[d]). Gregory Herek, professor. Retrieved from http://psychology.ucdavis.edu/herek/#Bio.

Herek, G. M. (n.d.[e]). Lesbians and gay men in the U.S. military: Historical background. Retrieved from http://psychology.ucdavis.edu/rainbow/html/military_history.html.

Herek, G. M. (n.d.[f]). One in five sexual minority adults have experienced a hate crime. Retrieved from http://psychology.ucdavis.edu/rainbow/html/hate_crimes_2007_study.html.

Herek, G. M. (n.d.[g]). Sexual prejudice: Prevalence. Retrieved from http://psychology.ucdavis.edu/rainbow/html/prej_prev.html.

Herek, G. M., & Capitanio, J. P. (1996). "Some of my best friends": Intergroup contact, concealable stigma, and heterosexuals' attitudes toward gay men and lesbians. *Personality and Social Psychology Bulletin, 22*, 412-424.

Homophobia. (n.d.). In Conservapedia. Retrieved from http://www.conservapedia.com/Homophobia.

Hooker, E. (1957). The Adjustment of the male overt homosexual. *Journal of Projective Techniques, 21*, 18.

Hooker, E. (1993). Reflections of a 40-year exploration: A scientific view on homosexuality. *American Psychologist, 48*(4), 450-453.

Intersex Society of North America. (n.d.[a]). How common is intersex? Retrieved from http://www.isna.org/faq/frequency.

Intersex Society of North America. (n.d.[b]). What does ISNA recommend for children with intersex? Retrieved from http://www.isna.org/faq/patient-centered.

Intersex Society of North America. (n.d[c]). Why is ISNA using "DSD"? Retrieved from http://www.isna.org/node/1066.

Irvine, J. M. (1991). *Disorders of desire: Sex and gender in modern American sexology.* Philadelphia, PA: Temple University Press.

Jhally, S. (Producer). (1999). *Tough guise.* Northampton, MA: Media Education Foundation.

Johnson, R. W. (1995). American psychology: The political science. *Collected papers from the NARTH annual conference, Saturday, 29 July 1995.* Retrieved from http://www.narth.com/docs/1995papers/johnson.html.

Kimmel, D. C., & Garnets, L. D. (2003). What a light it shed: The life of Evelyn Hooker. In L. D. Garnets & D. C. Kimmel (Eds.), P*sychological perspectives on lesbian,* *gay, and bisexual experiences* (pp. 31-49). New York: Columbia University Press.

Kinsey, A., et al. (1948). *Sexual behavior in the human male.* Bloomington, IN: Indiana University Press.

The Kinsey Institute for Sex, Gender, and Reproduction. (n.d.). Facts about Kinsey, the film. Retrieved from http://www.kinseyinstitute.org/about/Movie-facts. html#data .

Lee, P. A., Houk, C. P., Ahmed, S. F., and Hughes, I. A. (2006). Consensus statement on management of intersex disorders. *Pediatrics, 118*(2), 488-500.

LeVay, S. (1991). A difference in hypothalamic structure between heterosexual and homosexual men. *Science, 253*(5023), 1034-1037.

LeVay, S. (1997). *Queer science: The use and abuse of research into homosexuality.* Cambridge: The MIT Press.

Lever, J. (1994, August 23). Sexual revelations: The 1994 *Advocate* survey of sexuality and relationships: The men. *The Advocate,* 17-24.

Lever, J. (1995, August 22). Lesbian sex survey: The 1995 *Advocate* survey of sexuality and relationships: The women. *The Advocate,* 22-30.

Levine, D. (2011, April 6). Gay judge never considered dropping Prop 8 case. *Reuters.* Retrieved from http://www.reuters.com/article/2011/04/06/us-gaymarriage-judge-idUSTRE7356TA20110406.

Levy, A. (2009, March 2). Lesbian nation: Why gay women took to the road. *The New Yorker*. Retrieved from http://www.newyorker.com/reporting/2009/03/02/090302fa_fact_levy#ixzz0t7FK5y2Y.

Liptak, A. (2008, May 16). California Supreme Court overturns gay marriage ban. *The New York Times*. Retrieved from http://www.nytimes.com/2008/05/16/us/16marriage.html.

Liu, S. (1998, July). Cheryl Chase. *Curve*. Retrieved from http://backup.curvemag.com/Detailed/77.html.

Marshall, E. (1995, June 30). NIH's "gay gene" study questioned. *Science*, *268*(5219), 1841.

Matier, P., & Ross, A. (2010, February 7). Judge being gay a non-issue during Prop 8 trial. *San Francisco Chronicle*. Retrieved from http://articles.sfgate.com/2010-02-07/bay-area/17848482_1_same-sex-marriage-sexual-orientation-judge-walker.

McCarn, S. R., & Fassinger, R. E. (1996). Revisioning sexual minority identity formation: A new model of lesbian identity and its implications for counseling and research. *The Counseling Psychologist*, *24*(3), 508-534.

McHugh. P. (2009). Surgical sex. Retrieved from http://www.firstthings.com/article/2009/02/surgical-sex--35.

Money, J. (1973). *Man and woman, boy and girl*. Baltimore, MD: The Johns Hopkins University Press.

Money, J. (1975). Ablatio penis: normal male infant sex-reassigned as a girl. *Archives of Sexual Behavior*, *4*(1), 65-71.

Money, J., and Tucker, P. (1975). *Sexual signatures: On being a man or a woman*. Boston, MA: Little, Brown.

Mustanski, B. S., et al. (2005). A genomewide scan of male sexual orientation. *Human Genetics*, *116*(4), 272-278.

Mosher, W. D., Chandra, A., & Jones, J. (2005). Sexual behavior and selected health measures: Men and women 15-44 years of age, United States, 2002. *Advance data from vital and health statistics*. Hyattsville, MD: National Center for Health Statistics.

National Association for Research and Therapy of Homosexuality. (n.d.[a]). Female homosexual development. Retrieved from http://www.narth.com/docs/FemaleHomosexualDevelopment.pdf.

National Association for Research and Therapy of Homosexuality. (n.d.[b]). Dr. Jeffrey Satinover testifies before Massachusetts Senate committee studying gay marriage. Retrieved from http://www.narth.com/docs/senatecommittee.html.

National Association for Research and Therapy of Homosexuality. (n.d.[c]). NARTH mission statement. Retrieved from http://narth.com/menus/mission.html.

Nicolosi, J. (1997). *Reparative therapy of male homosexuality: A new clinical approach*. Lanham, MD: Jason Aronson.

Nicolosi, L. A. (2009). New journal article makes the case for reorientation therapy. Retrieved from http://www.narth.com/docs/casefor.html.

Nimmons, D. (1994, March 1). Sex and the brain. *Discover*. Retrieved from http://discovermagazine.com/1994/mar/sexandthebrain346/?searchterm=simon%20levay.

1964 Civil Rights Act. (n.d.). Retrieved from http://www.historylearningsite.co.uk/1964_civil_rights_act.htm.

No on 8. (2008, October 30). Discrimination. Retrieved from http://www.youtube.com/watch?v=Oj-0-xMrsyxE.

O'Brien, W. (2007, May 31). A pride trans-formation: D.C.'s trans community organizes its first dedicated Capital Pride event. Retrieved from http://www.metroweekly.com/gauge/?ak=2745.

Ochs, R. (1996). Biphobia: It goes more than two ways. In B. A. Firestein (Ed.), *Bisexuality: The psychology and politics of an invisible minority* (pp. 217-239). Thousand Oaks, CA: Sage.

Oii Australia. (n.d.). A Conspiracy of Deceit: Alice Dreger, ISNA, the invention of DSD and Dix Poppas of Cornell who cuts up intersex babies' clitorises. Retrieved from http://oiiaustrailia.com/media/articles/conspiracy-deceit-alice-dreger-isna-invention-dsds-dix-poppas-cornell-cuts-intersex-babies-clitorises.

Otjen, J. P., et al. (1993). Summary report of the Military Working Group on recommended Department of Defense homosexual policy. In R. M Baird & M. K. Baird (Eds.), *Homosexuality: Debating the issues* (pp. 158-170). Amherst, NY: Prometheus Press.

Pattatucci-Aragon, A. (2001) Contra la corriente (Against the current). In N. K. Gartrell & E. D. Rothblum (Eds.), *Everyday Mutinies: Funding Lesbian Activism* (pp. 1-14). New York: Harrington Park Press.

Pilkington, N. W., & D'Augelli, A. R. (1995). Victimization of lesbian, gay, and bisexual youth in community settings. *Journal of Community Psychology, 23,* 33-55.

Portrait of a gay gene. (1997, October). *Discover.* Retrieved from http://rex.nci.nih.gov/RESEARCH/basic/biochem/DiscoverArticle.html.

Pride South Florida. (n.d.). History of Pride South Florida. Retrieved from http://www.pridesouthflorida.org/faq.htm.

Proposition 8 commercial. (2008, October 25). Retrieved from http://www.youtube.com/watch?v=75J3TN9Zzck&NR=1.

ProtectMarriage.com. (2008, September 29). Yes on 8 TV ad: Whether you like it or not. Retrieved from http://www.youtube.com/watch?v=4kKn5LNhNto&feature=related.

ProtectMarriage.com. (2008, October 20). Yes on

8 TV ad: Everything to do with schools. Retrieved from http://www.youtube.com/watch?v=7352ZVMKBQM&feature=related.

ProtectMarriage.com. (2008, October 25). Prop. 8 ad: Gay marriage is BEING TAUGHT already. Retrieved from http://www.youtube.com/watch?v=7lNdA1mlWw0.

Raymond, J. (1979). *The transsexual empire: The making of the she-male*. Boston, MA: Beacon Press.

Reagan, R. (1978, November 1). Editorial: Two ill-advised California trends. *Los Angeles Herald-Examiner*, A19.

Rosik, C. H., & Byrd, A. D. (2007). Marriage and the civilizing of male sexual nature. *American Psychologist*, *62(7)*, 711-712.

Sailer, S. (2002, August 26). Q&A with J. Michael Bailey: The science of sexual orientation. Retrieved from http://www.isteve.com/2002_QA_J._Michael_Bailey.htm.

San Diego Superior Court (1994). *Merino v. Boy Scouts*.

San Francisco Pride. (n.d.). Retrieved from http://www.sfpride.org/.

Satinover, J. B. (n.d.). The "Trojan couch": How the mental health associations misrepresent science. Retrieved from http://www.narth.com/docs/TheTrojanCouchSatinover.pdf.

Savin-Williams, R. C. (2005). *The new gay teenager.* Cambridge, MA: Harvard University Press.

Savin-Williams, R. C., & Diamond, L. M. (1997). Sexual orientation as a developmental context for lesbians, gays, and bisexuals: Biological perspectives. In N.L. Segal, G.E. Weisfeld, & C.C. Weisfeld, (Eds.), *Uniting psychology and biology: Integrative perspectives on human development* (pp. 217-238). Washington, D.C.: American Psychological Association Press.

Schmiechen, R. (Producer). (1992). *Changing our minds: The story of Evelyn Hooker.* San Francisco, CA: Frameline.

Schwartz, J. (2010, August 5). Conservative jurist, with independent streak. *The New York Times.* Retrieved from http://www.nytimes.com/2010/08/06/us/06walker.html?_r=1&ref=vaughn_r_walker/.

Scolar, S. (2001). Pat Califia – a three-part interview. Retrieved from http://www.technodyke.com/features/patcalifa4.asp#shosho.

Secretary of State (1978). *Statement of Vote.* State of California.

Sheff, E. (in press). Children's welfare in polyamorous families. *Journal of Family Issues.*

Sherif, M. (1958). Superordinate goals in the reduction of intergroup conflict. *American Journal of Sociology, 63*(4), 349-356.

Shiller, V. M. (2007). Science and advocacy issues in research on children of gay and lesbian parents. *American Psychologist*, *62*(7), 712-713.

Socarides, C. (1995). *Homosexuality: A freedom too far.* Roberkai.

Supreme Court of California. (2004, August 12). *Lockyer v. City and County of San Francisco.* Retrieved from http://scholar.google.com/scholar_case?case=2060307963634374123&hl=en&as_sdt=2&as_vis=1&oi=scholarr.

Transgender London. (2010). Psychological damage. Retrieved from http://transgenderlondon.com/Pychological%20Damage.htm.

Transsexual Road Map. (n.d.[a]). Clarke Institute. Retrieved from http://www.tsroadmap.com/info/clarke-institute.html.

Transsexual Road Map. (n.d.[b]). Dean Hamer on transsexualism. Retrieved from http://www.tsroadmap.com/info/dean-hamer.html.

Transsexual Road Map. (n.d.[c]). J. Michael Bailey and eugenics. Retrieved from http://www.tsroadmap.com/info/bailey-eugenics.html.

Transsexual Road Map. (n.d.[d]). Selected trans published resources. Retrieved from http://www.tsroadmap.com/info/books.html.

Transsexual Road Map. (n.d.[e]). Simon LeVay on transsexualism. Retrieved from http://www.tsroadmap.com/info/simon-levay.html.

Troiden, R. R. (1989). The formation of homosexual identities. *Journal of Homosexuality*, *17*(1-2), 43-74.

TruthWinsOut. (n.d.). Retrieved from http://www.truth-winsout.org/our-vision/.

United States Court of Appeals, Eighth Circuit. (1998). *Brandon v. Lotter*. Retrieved from http://caselaw.find-law.com/us-8th-circuit/1350283.html.

United States Department of Defense. (n.d.). Don't ask, don't tell education training. Retrieved from https://kb.defense.gov/app/answers/detail/a_id/705/~/don't-ask,-don't-tell-education-and-training.

United States District Court for the Northern District of California. (2010, August 4). *Perry v. Schwarzenegger*. Retrieved from https://ecf.cand.uscourts.gov/cand/09cv2292/files/09cv2292-ORDER.pdf.

United States Supreme Court. (1954). *Brown v. Board of Education*. Retrieved from http://caselaw.lp.findlaw.com/scripts/getcase.pl?court=US&vol=347&invol=483.

U. S. Government Printing Office. (1996, September 21). Public Law 104-199 – Defense of Marriage Act. Retrieved from http://www.gpo.gov/fdsys/pkg/PLAW-104publ199/content-detail.html.

Vogel, L. (2006). Michigan Womyn's Music Festival sets the record "straight." Retrieved from http://femi-nism.org/michigan/20060822-mwmf.txt.

WEDDINGS/CELEBRATIONS: Dean Hamer, Joseph

Wilson. (2004, April 11). *The New York Times*. Retrieved from http://www.nytimes.com/2004/04/11/style/weddings-celebrations-dean-hamer-joseph-wilson.html.

Weil, E. (2006, September 24). What if it's (sort of) a boy and (sort of) a girl? *The New York Times*. Retrieved from http://www.nytimes.com/2006/09/24/magazine/24intersexkids.html.

White, H. (2007, July 16). The mother of the homosexual movement – Evelyn Hooker, Ph.D. Retrieved from http://www.lifesitenews.com/news/archive/ldn/2007/jul/07071603.

Willis, S. (Producer). (1993, July 15). *Nightline*. Nashville, TN: Vanderbilt University Television News Archive.

Wood, J. M., Nezworski, M. T., Lilienfeld, S. O., & Garb, H. N. (2003). *What's wrong with the Rorschach? Science confronts the controversial inkblot test*. San Francisco, CA: Jossey-Bass.

Zhou, J., Hofman, M. A., Gooren, L. J. G., and Swaab, D. F. (1995). A sex difference in the human brain and its relation to transsexuality. *Nature, 378*, 68-70.

INDEX

A

Accord Alliance, 150

acquired immune deficiency syndrome (AIDS), INAH-3 and, 23-24

activist research, 179-181, 197-198, 216

Addams, Calpernia, 131

adjustment, of homosexual men, Hooker research and, 164-175

"The Adjustment of the Male Overt Homosexual" (Hooker), 17, 166

advocacy science, 197-198

AIDS. *See* acquired immune deficiency syndrome

AIS. *See* androgen insensitivity syndrome

Allen, Laura, 20-21

Allport, Gordon, 202-203, 208, 212, 221

altruism, 228-229

AMA. *See* American Medical Association

Amendment 2, Colorado, 43-44, 50, 211

American Beauty (movie), 182

American Medical Association (AMA), gay activism and, 18

American Psychiatric Association (APA)

   DSM diagnosis of homosexuality, 14-19, 167, 168, 171-174

   gay activism and, 17-18, 171-172

American Psychological Association (APA)

   "don't ask, don't tell" policy and, 194-195

   resolution against homosexual discrimination, 173

B

ABOUT THE AUTHOR

Gayle E. Pitman, Ph.D. is a clinical psychologist and Professor of Psychology at Sacramento City College. She has conducted research on the physical and mental health of lesbian women, and she has written numerous articles and book chapters on gender and sexual orientation. She lives in Northern California.

Made in the USA
Charleston, SC
26 September 2011